Christianity

and the Arts

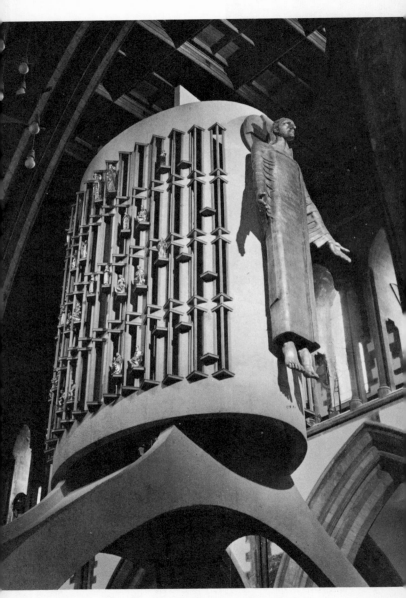

Fig. 1. Epstein: *Majestas*.

Christianity and the Arts

DONALD WHITTLE
Homerton College, Cambridge

FORTRESS PRESS   PHILADELPHIA

Published in Great Britain in 1966
by A. R. Mowbray & Co., Ltd., London

© A. R. MOWBRAY & CO., LTD., 1966

Published in the United States in
1967 by Fortress Press,
Philadelphia

Library of Congress Catalog Card No. 67-15024

Printed in the U.S.A.

4155A67   1-202

Contents

List of Illustrations

Acknowledgements

THE thanks of the author and the publishers are due to the following for permission to reproduce photographs. No. 1, Stanley Travers; Nos. 2, 8, 9, 11, 12, The Mansell Collection; No. 3, Albertina Verlag, Vienna; No. 4, Country Life Ltd.; Nos. 5, 15, Ralph Meakins; Nos. 6, 23, The Provost and Chapter of Coventry; Nos. 7, 13, The National Gallery; No. 10, Arthur Tooth & Sons Ltd. and the Tate Gallery; No. 14, Methodist Education Committee; No. 16, Whitworth Art Gallery; No. 17 Chester Beatty Collection; No. 18, Edward D. Mills; No. 19, Mrs. Reves and The Worshipful Company of Goldsmiths.

THE thanks of the author and the publishers are due to the following for permission to quote extracts: The Abingdon Press, *Contemporary Theatre and the Christian Faith* by K. Baxter; Messrs. Allen and Unwin Ltd., *The Creative Imagination* by K. Barnes; The Architectural Press, *Towards a Christian Architecture* by P. Hammond; Messrs. Barnes and Co., *Music and the European Mind* by Wilfrid Dunwell; Messrs. Barrie and Rockliffe, *Liturgy and Architecture* by P. Hammond; Messrs. Chatto and Windus and Mrs. Laura Huxley, *On Arts and Artists* by Aldous Huxley, also the same publishers and Mrs. Willa Muir, *Autobiography* by Edwin Muir; Rosica Colin Ltd., *Waiting for Godot* by Samuel Beckett; Messrs. W. Collins

Sons and Co. Ltd., *Five Minutes to Twelve* by W. B. J. Martin, and *The Novelist and the Passion Story* by F. W. Dillistone; Messrs. Coward-McCann Inc., *Lord of the Flies* by William Golding; Messrs. Doubleday and Co. Ltd., *A Kind of Loving* by Stan Barstow; Messrs. Duckworth and Co. Ltd., *The Church and Music* by Erik Routley; The Faith Press, *Christianity and the Visual Arts* ed. G. Cope; Messrs. Farrar, Straus and Giroux, *Poetry and Drama* by T. S. Eliot; The Fortress Press, *Church Music and Theology* by Erik Routley; The Grove Press, *Rhinoceros* by Eugene Ionesco; Messrs. Harcourt, Brace and World Inc., *Collected Poems* (1909–1962), *Four Quartets*, *Murder in the Cathedral* and *The Cocktail Party*, by T. S. Eliot, *Autumn Journal* by Louis MacNeice, *Pincher Martin* and *The Brass Butterfly* by William Golding; Messrs. Hill and Wang, *The Angry Theater* by J. R. Taylor; Messrs. Hodder and Stoughton, *Images of God* by A. C. Bridge; Messrs. Houghton Mifflin, *Collected Poems* by A. MacLeish and *The Less Deceived* by P. Larkin; Messrs. Macmillan, *Christian Church Art* by McClinton; New Directions Inc., and The Literary Executors of the Dylan Thomas Estate, *Collected Poems* by Dylan Thomas; The Oxford University Press, *Collected Poems* by E. Muir and *Twentieth Century Church Music* by Erik Routley; The Phaidon Press, *Grünewald* by Huysmans; Messrs. S. and G. Phillips, *Look Back in Anger* by John Osborne; Random House Inc., *The Whitsun Weddings* by Philip Larkin; Messrs. Thames and Hudson, *A Concise History of Art* by Bazin; Messrs. A. Tiranti Ltd., *Architectural Principles* by Wittkower; The University of Chicago Press, *Before Philosophy* by H. and H. A. Frankfort; The Viking Press, *A View from the Bridge* by Arthur Miller, *Brighton Rock*, *The Heart of the Matter* and *The Power and the Glory* by Graham Greene, *Collected Poems* by D. H. Lawrence; The Westminster Press, *Rembrandt and the Gospel* by W. A. Visser t'Hooft.

Thanks are also due to A. C. Bridge and *The Listener* (Dec. 6th 1962); also to *A Review of English Literature* for permission to quote from Dr. Peter Green's article 'The World of William Golding; and to *St. Martin's Review* (1958) for permission to quote from an article by G. Pace.

In addition the author would like to acknowledge his debt to a series of talks on contemporary literature in the B.B.C. 'The Christian Religion and its Philosophy' series for Sixth Forms, and to an article by Joseph Sittler in *The Student World*, No. 2, 1955.

Should any acknowledgement have been omitted inadvertently, then this oversight will be rectified in subsequent editions if brought to the attention of either the author or the publishers.

Preface

THIS BOOK sets out to explore the important but intricate relationship between Christianity and the arts. There is a tendency, in so wide a field, either to over-simplify what is highly complex or to become so involved with detail as to be obscure. In general, I have tried to select a few examples in each domain and deal with these at some length so as to highlight the main points at issue.

This method leaves obvious gaps and it is hoped that the reader can fill some of these from his own knowledge and interest. With the exception of the chapters on the visual arts and music, my concern has been almost exclusively with works of the present century and this book claims in no sense to be an exhaustive treatment of the subject. For those who wish to explore a particular field in more detail, the bibliography offers some guidance for further reading.

I would like to acknowledge the constant encouragement and help of the Editor of this series, Mr. Ridley Lewis; the helpful suggestions of my former colleague, Mr. J. B. Nellist and Mr. Don Saliers, of Yale, with particular reference to the chapters on painting, architecture and poetry; and the invaluable help of my wife in preparing the manuscript for the press.

The origin of this book is a series of discussions which, as Chaplain, I shared with members of the sixth form at

Ashville College. It is dedicated to those who endured, and perhaps enjoyed, that course. Certainly without them it would never have been written.

DONALD C. G. WHITTLE

Cambridge, 1966

1. Prologue

The soul of Man must quicken to creation.
Out of the formless stone, when the artist united himself with
    stone,
Spring always new forms of life, from the soul of man that is
    joined to the soul of stone;
Out of the meaningless practical shapes of all that is living or
    lifeless
Joined with the artist's eye, new life, new form, new colour.
Out of the sea of sound the life of music,
Out of the slimy mud of words, out of the sleet and hail of
    verbal imprecisions,
Approximate thoughts and feelings, words that have taken
    the place of thoughts and feelings,
There spring the perfect order of speech, and the beauty of
    incantation.

                  (T. S. Eliot, *The Rock*)

Momentarily to every man comes the crossing of the wires
with reality. It may be the Caliban moment—'This isle is full
of noises, sounds and sweet airs'—lost in a flash; or held a
little while in utter bliss, remembered and sometimes written
down: Saints in contemplation. . . . Bach working at the key-
board. . . . Fra Angelico working on the San Marco frescoes.
. . . Einstein working out the notion of relativity . . . they all
knew it. This is a kind of spiritual nuclear fission.

                  (Lawrence Lee)

THESE TWO men, trying to describe their experience as
creative artists, see that experience as a religious activity.
This is not surprising when we remember that the opening
chapter of the Bible is a poem about creation, the creation

B

of a universe which God saw to be good. Indeed both the
Old and the New Testaments begin with a description of
the two greatest Acts of God—the Creation and the
Incarnation. The earth is given to man for his enjoyment
and delight; form and content are perfectly fused in the
Word made flesh. Degas' statement that 'everything,
everything in this world has a sacred meaning' reminds us
of the Bible's assertion that in the Creation, God saw that
all that He had made was good. And it is from this
creation that the artist selects his raw material, his subject
matter, and transforms it by bestowing on it what the
poet Valéry called 'harmonious and unforgettable shape.'

There is every justification therefore for Christians to
take seriously the world of the artist, and this springs from
these two fundamental doctrines. The doctrine of Creation implies that God is sovereign over both the spiritual
and the material, and it is inevitable that the artist is
dealing with the things of God in so far as he observes
and interprets that creation. This doctrine, as worked out
in the Old Testament, also implies that the power and
majesty of God is to be seen in His imposition of order
upon chaos, and this is the function alike of both Creator
and creative artist. The artist has to wrestle with the
material, be it paint and canvas, stone, or language,
though he must also respect this material. 'It is the
function of all art to give us some perception of an order
in life, by imposing an order upon it.'[1]

The doctrine of the Incarnation speaks of the love of
God, relating Him to the personal struggle of man. Thus
whenever this action of God is explored and portrayed,
God's Word, Jesus Christ, is being unveiled. The totality

[1] *Poetry and Drama*, T. S. Eliot (Faber), p. 33

of the Christian Gospel springs from these two affirmations and is nowhere more clearly expressed than in the writings of St. Paul. All things are of Christ, in Him all the fulness of the created order dwells, and therefore the whole of life is sacramental—and it is the arts which enrich this life as they reveal both the order and the discord that are present in the world.

This book attempts to explore various ways in which artists, particularly those of the present generation, are able to express, through their work, their understanding of the human situation and the great Christian themes of man's relationship with God. In this introductory chapter we shall try to define the ways in which we can speak of 'Christian' and 'religious' art, and look at some of the problems which are raised by the use of images and symbols.

The relationships between Christian belief, the artist, and his work are intricate and complex. Generalizations are dangerous, especially in the field of aesthetics, but for the purpose of our present discussion we must make a general distinction, with respect to Christian art, along the following lines:

1. 'Christian art' can be regarded as an historical category. The term would then apply only to those works whose thematic material is overtly Christian—paintings of Biblical scenes, musical settings of religious texts, figures of Biblical characters, and literature dealing with the main themes of Christian belief.

2. The term can also be used in a wider sense as indicating some connection between a work of art and a Christian vision and understanding of the world. Some

novels, plays, paintings, etc., may be said to share in the
Christian vision even if they have no explicit Christian
references.

3. We can also define Christian art as a re-enactment
of creation. In this case, all works of art, whatever their
subject matter, and whatever the attitude of the artist,
can be seen as sheer imaginative works of creation, and as
such, reflections of the conviction that God created man
to be, in his own turn, a creator.

If an interpretation of Christian art along these lines is
accepted, it will not seem surprising, for instance, that for
some years a number of theological seminaries in America
have included in their curricula an intensive study of
such authors as D. H. Lawrence, Franz Kafka, and
William Faulkner, alongside the more expected disciplines
of Biblical studies and theology. This reflects the fact that
modern literature is often preoccupied with religious
concerns—not just in the work of the acknowledged
Christian writers such as Eliot, Greene, and others, but
in some of the most influential authors who are not to be
thought of as professing any formal religious allegiance.
Indeed we can often find the basic and ultimate religious
questions concerning man and his predicament more
powerfully and illuminatingly discussed by non-Christian
writers than by the orthodox believers, including the
theologians. Ours is an age of anxiety, in which men
have been forced to raise fundamental questions about
human existence, and the literature of our age inevitably
tends towards religious concerns.

In the definitions of Christian art given above we have
indicated that the term cannot be limited to those works
which either deal with a specifically Biblical subject or are

produced by committed Christians. Yet it is difficult to disperse the commonly held view that a religious film, for instance, must be either a Hollywood Biblical epic, or the life of a saint or martyr; that a religious novel must be an imaginary account of New Testament times, like *The Robe*; or a religious play must be a dramatic presentation of either the Nativity or the Passion. A film about the New York waterfront, a novel about a drowning sailor from a torpedoed ship, and a play set in sophisticated Mayfair can all be profoundly religious works, far nearer to the faith which the New Testament sets forth than the many works which are placed firmly in Biblical or ecclesiastical settings of the first century. It often happens that they are not only greater works when considered in the light of Christian discrimination, but also finer works of art, judged, as they must be, on their own merits as film, fiction, or drama. Bad art, like insincere religion, is intolerable to God and men alike. I do not want to labour this point here. It is amply developed in subsequent chapters. I stress it briefly now since it must be established that when we discuss the relationship between Christianity and the arts we are not limiting the field to what we might imperfectly describe as 'Church art', but are dealing with the whole texture and fabric of human experience, of which what men call 'religious experience' is only a part.

Historically, there have been strong links between religion and art. 'Art serves religion, and religion feeds art,' wrote Susan Langer. It has not always been a mutually acceptable collaboration. There have been periods in history when religious intolerance has threatened the human spirit, driving artists away from the Church—often the main source of their inspiration; at other times religion has become so submerged by sentimentality that the artist could not consider it worthy of his attention. Conversely, art has on occasions isolated itself, as happened during the Renaissance, when the artist developed a new consciousness of himself and his work. Some of the fluctuations in this relationship are developed later in the book and we need only mention them here. What we can appreciate is that in the modern scene there is more dialogue and confrontation between Christians and artists than we may have suspected, and this is as it should be. For if the Christian faith is concerned with God's dealings with men and men's relationships with one another, then it cannot ignore any serious comment on the human situation. An appreciation of modern art not only helps us to understand our culture—it involves us in an examination of ultimate questions about man.

Images and Symbols

> A world ends when its metaphor has died.
> An age becomes an age, all else beside,
> When sensuous poets in their pride invent
> Emblems for the soul's consent
> That speak the meanings men will never know
> But man-imagined images can show:
> It perishes when those images, though seen,
> No longer mean. . . .

Thus Archibald MacLeish expresses the dilemma of the artist in an age when traditional images and symbols are dying, and when there is no generally accepted Christian culture within which the Church and the artist can meet in confidence and empathy. It is not only the artists who are aware of the difficulty. Paul Tillich, the theologian, argues that many Christians are often 'unaware of the numinous power inherent in genuine symbols, words, acts, persons, things. They have replaced the great wealth of symbols appearing in the Christian tradition by rational concepts, moral laws, and subjective emotions.' Tillich distinguishes carefully between a sign and a symbol. Both are alike in that they point beyond themselves to something else. But unlike the sign, the symbol has its significance because of the reality to which it points. For example, red, amber and green traffic lights are 'signs'; they point beyond themselves to the necessity for cars to stop or proceed; but a national flag is a symbol, for it participates in that which it represents. If a loyal patriot is ordered by the enemy to spit on his country's flag, he will not do this, for the flag itself participates in the notions of loyalty, honour, national pride of that country. It is more than a sign.

The main function of the symbol, however, is to open up levels of reality which are otherwise hidden and cannot be grasped in any other way. So the symbolism in poetry, visual art, or music, reveals to us levels of reality which can be opened up in no other way. And because they do this they cannot be replaced by other symbols. Tillich points out that we could, for example, change the traffic lights to blue instead of green (if circumstances demanded it) and they would still be effective 'signs.' The Highway Code would simply inform us that blue meant 'Go.' But we cannot change a symbolic word, like 'God.' It cannot be replaced when used in its special function.

This apparent digression into the meaning of symbols is important, for it is necessary to be clear that some

symbols no longer have the same power and significance
for human life that they once had, and they are, in this
sense, dead. Some of them have ceased to speak because
the New Testament world from which they sprang is not
our world. The instructed Christian may know, by association, what is meant when we speak of Christ as 'The
Lamb of God,' or 'The Bread of Life'; but this would
have little relevance for someone living in a culture where
lambs were never seen except as mutton, or bread was
not the staple diet. This concern for the failure of symbols
has led some thinkers, such as Bultmann, to suggest that
the Christian message needs freeing entirely from those
modes of expression and thought which are no longer
readily understood. When these outdated symbols are
used in religious art they only succeed in confusing rather
than communicating the message. Thus the detailed
symbolism of the four beasts in the tapestry in Coventry
Cathedral is too obscure to make an immediate impact on
those who see it, and a guidebook explanation is needed
to interpret their significance. The symbols are no longer
meaningful.

It is not only the visual symbol which has lost its power.
The poet is also faced with the problem of imagery. The
symbolic words in Protestant theology for the saving work
of Christ, words like justification, redemption, ransom,
and salvation, are effective symbols no more. This is
painfully evident in popular hymns, some of which are
not only obscure to modern man but frankly offensive:

> There is a fountain filled with blood
> Drawn from Immanuel's veins;
> And sinners, plunged beneath that flood,
> Lose all their guilty stains.

When T. S. Eliot attempts to describe this saving work in terms which will speak to the modern reader, he writes of a hospital where the values are all reversed:

> The wounded surgeon plies the steel
> That questions the distempered part;
> Beneath the bleeding hands we feel
> The sharp compassion of the healer's art
> Resolving the enigma of the fever chart.
>
> Our only health is the disease
> If we obey the dying nurse
> Whose constant care is not to please
> But to remind of our, and Adam's curse,
> And that, to be restored, our sickness must grow worse.
>
> The whole earth is our hospital
> Endowed by the ruined millionaire,
> Wherein, if we do well, we shall
> Die of the absolute paternal care
> That will not leave us, but prevents us everywhere.
>
> The chill ascends from feet to knees,
> The fever sings in mental wires.
> If to be warmed, then I must freeze
> And quake in frigid purgatorial fires
> Of which the flame is roses, and the smoke is briars.
>
> The dripping blood our only drink,
> The bloody flesh our only food:
> In spite of which we like to think
> That we are sound, substantial flesh and blood—
> Again, in spite of that, we call this Friday good.
>
> *(East Coker IV)*

Eliot's poetry is full of images of paradox, but so is the Christian faith from which it springs. Jesus talked of losing life in order to save it, of dying in order to live; and so in this poetic hospital the patients go not to get better, but to die. This death, however, is not the exit from life but the entrance, the new life born of the love of God, that 'absolute paternal care that will not leave us, but prevents us everywhere.' Mankind, suffering the curse of Adam, the ruined millionaire, is delivered by the surgeon, Christ, aided by the nurse, the Church. And what we think is our substantial material life in the flesh is ghostly compared with the life offered by Christ in his self-giving on Good Friday.

It is clear from this brief exposition that Eliot's imagery is not completely transformed, and the power of the words associated with the traditional myths and symbols (like Adam, the Healer, flesh, blood, Good Friday) is essential to a full understanding of the poem. Indeed, this raises the question as to how far Christian art can cut itself off from its roots in the past. It must dissociate itself from what grew on the traditional roots, if that growth was superfluous; but Christianity is essentially a faith rooted in an historical event, and this event has been remembered and nourished in an unbroken tradition through the ages. In every generation and changing culture new shoots will burst forth from the old roots.

The peculiar difficulty facing the modern artist is well expressed by Anthony Bridge, both artist and theologian, when he reminds us that 'since we live in an age immediately following one in which all conventional imagery died, and the main stream of European art petered out into a wilderness of dead formulae, the greatest force at work upon a creative artist is one that drives him away from any image associated with this nineteenth-century

graveyard. For Picasso this is liberating and invigora-
ting. He can produce his tremendous images of modern
dissolution. *Guernica* was as radically remote as it could
have been from any imagery which might possibly have
been associated with the corpse of the Renaissance
tradition. But once an artist has to paint a Christ-figure,
or an architect has to build a church, he is faced with a
subject that is inevitably closely associated with post-
Renaissance imagery. Everyone's mind is a junk shop of
dead Christian images: of nightgowned figures of Jesus
in sentimental poses, of desperate wax Madonnas, of
awkward or ungainly church furniture, and of stained
glass looking like an advertisement for ruby port. Artists
are no exception to this rule. Their minds, too, turn away
in disgust from these persistent associations; and as a
result the great majority of them simply do not contemplate working on Christian subjects or themes. Those
who do are subjected to an inevitably self-conscious quest
of an acceptable image; and self-consciousness in the arts
is a major disability.'[1]

The Christian artist in any age faces a double demand:
a faithfulness to his artistic discipline, the anguish of sheer
craftsmanship and creation that is required of all artists;
and faithfulness to his religious perception, his awareness
of the ultimate meaning of life. It will become clear, in
the course of this book, that the terms 'Christian' and
'Artist' are not mutually exclusive. It is true that some
sectors of the Church have inhibitions about the arts,
tolerating them with a disapproving eye and only on rare
occasions allowing them to intrude into Christian worship. Yet when modern art expresses so well, and with

[1] *The Listener*, 6 Dec., 1962

such pathos, the human condition of man without God, or when an Epstein brings us to our knees with the majesty of the carved Christ, we may surely see such art as the work of the Holy Spirit, bringing both judgment and glory, and helping us to share with one another our deepest convictions and longings about ourselves, our world, and our destiny.

2. Painting

The Image of Christ

FAMOUS PEOPLE'S names often conjure up mental images of their appearance, and if they are personalities of this century we shall probably have some photographic or cartoon-type image: Churchill with his cigar; Hitler and his lock of hair and moustache; the sharp features of Kennedy. Those who lived before the age of mass media may be fixed in our imagination by some well-known portrait: Holbein's *Henry VIII*, or Napoleon, his arm tucked inside his great-coat. But what of Jesus of Nazareth? What picture do we have of him? For some it may be the sentimental conception of many illustrated Bibles or the popular, if somewhat suspect, portrait of an anaemic, pale-faced Galilean which adorns the walls of many Sunday schools and classrooms. For others, according to taste and experience, it might be the smooth-limbed, suspended figure of Dali's *Christ of St. John of the Cross*, or the *Majestas* by Epstein at Llandaff (fig. 1), or Sutherland's tapestry *Christ Enthroned in Glory* at Coventry (fig. 6).

Do we need to visualize a human face when we think of Jesus? Certainly the writers of the Gospels did not seem to think their readers would want to know about his appearance. They tell us nothing of his features, his voice, how he dressed (as they do for John the Baptist), and little about his family and friends. This lack of interest in the physical features of Jesus of Nazareth is not surprising when we realize that the evangelists were not concerned primarily, if at all, in writing biographies of their hero; they were proclaiming Jesus as the Christ, the Son of God, and whether he was tall or short, dark or fair, was irrelevant to their purpose.

Yet European art in the Christian era was, until the later Renaissance, intimately bound up with the presentation of Christ in visual terms—either in drawings, paintings, sculpture, stained glass, mosaics, or tapestry. The subject of these works of art was either the person of Christ seen in one of the incidents from his recorded life, or some other Biblical event from the Old or New Testaments. The history of Christian art provides us, therefore, with a record of the way in which the person of Jesus was viewed in different periods and from differing backgrounds. At one time we may be looking at a very human Jesus of Galilee, at another at a representation of God the Son, reigning in triumph; in one Madonna and Child we may be faced with a 'grown-up' baby, strangely distorted, in another simply a beautiful drawing of any mother and her child; in one Crucifixion we see a man suffer, cruelly twisted in agony, in another a passive, almost remote figure reigns from the tree. Some of these differences arise from limitations of the artist's technique in a particular period but they also arise because art reflects the ethos of the society in which it is produced, and we can learn a good deal about the religious ethos of a society by studying its art.

In this chapter we shall compare pictures from different periods which show this change of thought and attitude taking place, and we shall then look at the way in which one particular incident, the Crucifixion, has been treated by six different artists. Our approach will therefore be

more wide ranging, historically, than in the sections on
literature where our main concern is with the work of
modern writers and their contemporary society.

The first three hundred years of the era saw a reluctance,
perhaps even an inability, on the part of Christians to
represent Jesus pictorially. There was, of course, the
strong inhibition of Hebrew tradition against any representational art. In the Old Testament graven images were
forbidden, for fear of idolatry, so that what artistic
inspiration existed among the Jews had been channelled
into elaborate patterning of a semi-abstract nature. The
first Christians made extensive use of symbols—the fish,
the lamb, and the cross were all fairly regular features of
the decoration of Christian tombs and places of worship.
If a pictorial image was made in this early period, Christ
would appear as a beardless Graeco-Roman youth, with
a halo—an Apollo-like Good Shepherd. Occasionally
there was a likeness to Orpheus, the demi-god who went
into the dark world of death and then returned. It was
from these tentative beginnings, fed by the influences of
Greek, Syrian, and Egyptian art, that the great age of
Byzantine art grew, to dominate European culture for
centuries to come.

The Byzantine Era

The Byzantine era became firmly established with the
recognition of Christianity by Constantine and the con-
sequent freedom for worship and the need to build, furnish
and decorate the many churches of that period. Christian
art concentrated not on any imaginary reconstruction of
the earthly Jesus of Nazareth, but on the assertion of St.
John that in Jesus, the Word was made flesh, and we

beheld his glory, as of the only begotten of the Father. Byzantine art, that is, was theological rather than representational, symbolic rather than naturalistic. The curly-haired beardless Greek boy of Ravenna changed, in time, to the bearded figure of Syro-Hittite heritage. Just as the Emperor was a God-like figure, awful and majestic, so Christ was depicted as Emperor of the Heavens, the Pantocrator, reigning over all in judgment and majesty.

The *Head of Christ* (fig. 2) is not a picture we look at in an art gallery; it faces the worshipper who enters the church at Cefalù in Sicily—a figure of tremendous power, set in mosaic in the apse, with the great gold background and the blue of Christ's cloak making an impressive impact on all who see it. It is as if we stand under the judgment of God, before the Word made flesh (the Word is held in Christ's left hand). One is surrounded by the saints and martyrs, the apostles and prophets, 'moving within a symbol of the Christian cosmos,' dominated by this all-powerful figure. And to the Byzantine civilization it represented one great truth. The men who had made this never thought that the Jesus who walked in Galilee looked at all like that, for this was not their concern. They wanted to express their faith that Jesus was no mere man, he was God, the majestic Son.

Early Renaissance

It is impossible within the scope of this book to indicate in detail the refinements and subdivisions of the main periods of painting, and the main sections used in this chapter are determined by the pictures selected for our study. Many might argue that Giotto was too early to be classed as a Renaissance painter but all would agree that

at the end of the thirteenth century a significant change
took place in Christian art and that Giotto is one of the
most important painters involved. This change could be
described as a progressive humanizing of the images. Both
painters and theologians were becoming more interested
than they had been for centuries in the humanity of
Christ, in his humility, and his gentleness rather than his
severity as Judge. The Byzantine culture had removed
Christ from men, making him remote and unapproach-
able. St. Francis of Assisi brought men a new vision of
Christ, the friend of children and sinners, the lover of
the animal world. 'Men were freer to look upon the
world and upon one another as manifestations of the
Creator . . . and this joy in the natural world was born of
an increasing confidence and of the knowledge that it was
God's creation and therefore a partial revelation of the
Divine.'[1]

At the artistic level, for the first time in a thousand
years, men showed an interest in the elements of Greek
naturalism and humanism from which Byzantine art had
been so rigidly purged. It was as if, in the Byzantine
period, Christian art 'had, slowly but surely, climbed
away from the alluring world of the senses, soaring ever
higher into a region of theological symbolism and, through
its images, carrying men's imagination to the transcendent
realm where the images hovered between God and man.'[2]
For a time Christian art retained this magnificent God-
centred quality. The great Romanesque cathedrals were
raised, hymns of praise in grey stone with rich, painstaking
carving undertaken with no thought of time or cost or

[1] *Christianity and the Visual Arts*, ed. G. Cope (Faith Press), p. 38
[2] *Images of God*, A. C. Bridge (H. & S.), p. 51

C

recognition. These men worshipped Christ the worshipful. But a change was taking place and in less than two
centuries men like Cimabue, Duccio, Giotto, and Masaccio
had transformed Christian iconography. 'They found it
a system of theological symbolism; they left it a system of
general symbolism, well adapted to the expression of a
humanist ethos and eminently capable of embodying the
reverence of the Church for the humanity of her Lord,
but no longer able to evoke the mystery or the majesty of
his divinity. In other words, they inherited a language of
Christian theology, and they translated it into the language of Christian humanism.'[1]

The method which Giotto used can be seen in *The
Betrayal* (fig. 8), a fresco in Padua where, incidentally,
the Byzantine traces remain in his general setting out of
the material. But whereas the Byzantine tradition showed
Christ as more than a man, Giotto portrays him as a
better man, more noble, more perfect than other men—
in this case, Judas. This is still not a representational
picture of Jesus of Nazareth, with the perfectly combed
hair and beard. But here is *the* man, as God meant man
to be and not as we really are because of our sin. But
there is far more to this picture than this aspect of the
representation of Christ. There is a powerful emotion
conveyed, both by the faces of the others, and by the form
in which they are arranged. One group moves from the
left hand side of the picture towards the head of Christ,
the other from the opposite side towards the head of
Judas. Above these two converging lines, the helmets of
the soldiers give solidity to these converging thrusts, while
the soldiers' staves radiate from the point of focus. And

[1] Ibid., p. 52

just where the two heads meet, the noses of two soldiers behind thrust forward almost as a wedge driven into the centre of the picture. The whole scene has a tension about it, as the perfect man, Jesus, meets his enemy.

Giotto, then, represents the beginning of a new era for Christian art in which Jesus is seen not as the Divine Word, the Son of God, but as a man. The West has never really diverged from this course, and as the Renaissance progressed, the representations of Christ came to be less concerned with his divinity, and more with his humanity, so that eventually artists were concerned only with humanity, with the beauty of the human form, with art produced not for the glory of God but for the glory of man. At the same time the artist was developing a new consciousness of himself and his work. Increasingly he separated himself from the craftsmen—architect from mason, painter from glazier, writer from scribe. It was this separation which led eventually to the isolation of the artist—and the titanism of the Renaissance.[1]

The Renaissance

This change in ways of portraying Christ can be clearly seen if we compare two interpretations of *Virgin and Child* (figs. 3, 4). Raphael has given us an exquisite drawing of a young woman and a young child. There is a serenity and peace about this picture—in its form and structure, in the still gaze of both mother and child on the pomegranate. We can look at this picture peacefully, for they are not looking at us; we look at them as observers from the outside. In the Russian Ikon, from the Byzantine

[1] Cf. *Dilemma of the Arts*, Weidlé (S.C.M.), pp. 12–13.

tradition, there is a symbolic rather than naturalist treatment of the figures—the child's head is regarded as the outward image of the indwelling God; Mary is seen not as a perfect young woman, the archetype of faithful motherhood, but as the *Theotokos*, the mother of God. Perhaps the most striking contrast is that we are drawn into the picture by the eyes of the mother and child which look out at us with a certain disturbing concern. We cannot, as with the Raphael, look at this scene from outside.

There are two points of comment which arise from these pictures. The first is that different ways of looking at God are expressed in them. For Raphael, and for his colleagues of the Renaissance, God was to be attained most nearly in human perfection. From the disorderly and unruly material of life, man seeks perfection in beauty, balance, and symmetry, and by looking at the most perfect quality possible in human experience we come closest to God. But for the painter of the ikon there is no search for human beauty and perfection—there is sorrow and implicit anguish in this couple rather than peace and tranquillity. For his work is a comment not only on the first part of the phrase in St. John's Gospel: 'The Word was made flesh,' but on the second: 'He dwelt among us as a light shining in the darkness.' Implicit in the Incarnation is the suffering Child, truly involved in the world's pain.

The second comment is concerned with the technique used by the artists. This cannot be divorced from the other but it is becoming clear as we look at the Raphael that there is an interest in drawing the human figure and taking delight in its proportions simply as a human figure.

Raphael expects us to admire the human body, the harmony of lines and colours, but he by no means demands the affirmation of our faith. At the sight of his *Transfiguration* Taine had to ask the question: 'In this miracle of his, does Raphael believe in anything at all?' And he answers: 'He believes above all that the accurate choice and arrangement of the figures is supremely important.'

In later periods, this tendency became more marked. In the *Virgin and Child* of Rubens we are conscious that Rubens, following the strong tendency to realism in the northern school, is using two of his friends as models for the virgin and child, and the baby with its curly hair and plump cheeks could well be Rubens' own son. And if we look at Tiepolo's study of the same theme, we see that the nativity has become 'demythologized' and in this process an important dimension has been lost. From this point on, the sentimental takes over and we are brought eventually to the sickly paintings of the Victorian period and the equally 'irreligious' Christmas card Madonnas of the present day.

The High Renaissance

It is impossible to give details of the varieties of schools of painting in the later Renaissance period. We can only hint at some of the features as they affect the presentation of Christ. There was an increasing tendency to paint Gospel incidents in the settings of the artist's own day, with Jesus as simply one person along with a number of others, and examples of this can be readily found in the works of painters like Bosch, Dürer, and Leonardo. The real interest in da Vinci's *Last Supper*, so frequently used in churches above the Holy Table, is not in the institution of that feast, but in the passionate inquiry among the disciples as to the identity of the betrayer: 'Lord, is it I?' There was also an attempt made by other painters—Michelangelo and Rubens for instance—to stress the unique character of Jesus by portraying him as a super-man, physically. Perhaps the most fitting symbol for the Renaissance is to be found in the great fresco of Michelangelo on the ceiling of the Sistine Chapel (fig. 11). Adam reaches out to his Creator and we are invited to revel in the glory of the human body; man, woken from his slumber, is reaching out for the divine spark of creativity so that he himself can become master and lord of the world.

The Reformation

The relationship between religion and art was profoundly affected by those two movements which link the medieval and the modern world—the Renaissance and the Reformation. The Renaissance, as we have seen, liberated man from imposed patterns and forms, and helped him to realize his power 'to create forms expressive of his deepest feelings in accordance with patterns of his own choosing. The Reformation was essentially a re-discovery of the right of the elect community—whether that community was a nation, a province, a city-state, or even a gathered group—to respond in its own deliberately chosen way to the manifestation of the sacred.'[1] The whole passion and drive of the Reformation focussed on the expression of the sacred through the *Word* rather than through any visual image. And man's response to that

[1] Cope, op. cit., p. 59

Word came 'through Cranmer's superb vernacular liturgies, Luther's incomparable biblical translations, Calvin's architectonic theological system—all worthy of the highest acclaim in the history of 'sacred art'. And it is not surprising that the form of art nearest to that of the word —namely that of the tone—was soon to find majestic expression in the works of J. S. Bach.'[1]

Although in many cases the visual arts had to seek for inspiration and patronage outside the boundaries of the Church, there were two figures in the sixteenth century whose works have a spiritual dimension lacking in most of their contemporaries, and they come from the two traditions that had separated in the turbulence of the Reformation—El Greco from Catholic Spain, and Rembrandt van Rijn from Reformed Holland. Luther himself, while being uninterested in the pomp and glitter of Baroque, thought that the Virgin should be portrayed to show 'how the exceeding riches of God joined in her with her utter poverty, the divine honour with her low estate, the divine glory with her shame . . . the divine greatness with her unworthiness.' Religious art would show the divine and sublime in what was lowly and contemptible.

It was Rembrandt who expressed what Luther desired. Still using the naturalism of the Renaissance, but with his particular technique of chiaroscuro, he depicted Christ as a servant, the Son of God become Man. His paintings reflect the concern of the Reformers with the personal relationship between an individual and God, and with the knowledge of God which is found in the common task, daily work, and family relationships.

[1] Cope, op. cit., p. 59

Until 1642 Rembrandt's life had been a series of successes. He had painted great Biblical themes, attracted by the dramatic and lively material they offered. In that year, however, his wife Saskia died, leaving him alone with his year-old son Titus. It was a time of great grief and loneliness and it had a profound effect on his painting. His self-portraits show a change from the self-assertive figure of the earlier period to one whose bearing speaks of suffering and loneliness. At the same time a new strength appears, and when he paints Biblical scenes it is with a new insight and simplicity of treatment which is a departure from the Baroque style, with its glorification of man. The Bible had at first appealed to Rembrandt because of the tension and movement in the dramatic stories; now he began to discover the message of the Bible. From 1642 onwards he no longer sought to exploit the Bible; he tried to interpret it. This change can be seen if we compare such subjects as *Ecce Homo* and *Christ at Emmaus* (fig. 9) painted both before and after this bereavement.

In his portrayal of Christ he stands alone against the splendour of seventeenth century Baroque. The Baroque Christ tends to become a super-man, a demi-god who has little in common with the real Christ, who had taken the form of a servant. In this an important insight is lost. For the glory can only come after and through the suffering. It was the achievement of Rembrandt to break free from the pressures of his world and to create a personal style of his own. It is a style full of tension, and necessarily so, for it had to proclaim the most contradictory of all messages: that God the Lord had become 'as any other man.' For Rembrandt the mystery of the Gospel consists

not in the glorification of man, but in the abasement of
God. So with great simplicity and reticence, rather than
with grand gesture, 'rather through suffering than through
glory, rather in quietude than in movement, we penetrate
to the divine mystery.'[1] It was to some extent the irony
of his age that his fellow-Protestants preferred the sensuous
appeal of Catholic Baroque.

Yet in the Catholic world a painter of great power and
originality was re-interpreting the life of Christ in forms
and style strange for his age. A native of Crete, El Greco
spent some years in Italy before settling in Spain. It
was in this later period that his work showed distinct
traces of Byzantine influences, especially in his delineation
of the features of Christ. In his *The Agony in the Garden*
(fig. 7) El Greco conveys the deep anguish of Jesus'
suffering in an interpenetration of forms and colours so
perfectly fused that the emotional qualities of the subject
are also qualities of the design itself. The outlines of the
rocks are twisted in an agonized way, as are the clouds
above. The sleeping apostles are enclosed, involved in
their own womb-like cave, whose outline is a continuation
of the spiralling movement which begins with the hem
of the angel's robe. And beyond the rock, which for the
moment shelters Christ, the soldiers approach, under an
apocalyptic lunar sky.

There is a sense in this, as in many of El Greco's
pictures, that the human figures are already caught up
with another world. 'Those faces with their uniformly
rapturous expression, those hands clasped in devotion or
lifted towards heaven, those figures stretched out to the
point where the whole inordinately elongated anatomy

[1] *Rembrandt and the Gospel*, W. A. Visser t'Hooft (S.C.M.), p. 115

becomes a living symbol of upward aspiration—all these
bear witness to the artist's constant preoccupation with
the ideas of mystical religion.'[1]

Baroque

We have already indicated that the changes in religious
art which came with the Renaissance could lead to art in
which, although there would still be no shortage of
religious subjects, the treatment would be humanist rather
than religious. That this was not always the case is
demonstrated by El Greco and Rembrandt, but they were
the exceptions. With the break up of society in the
Renaissance, artists began to look outside the church for
their patronage and their subject matter, and what church
art there was (and this was largely Catholic art) became
more and more florid and lachrymose, descending to the
self-consciousness of Reni and Ducci, to what Eric Gill
described as 'pink emetics,' to the art for propaganda's
sake of the Baroque, to art no longer to the true glory of
God. Baroque church art is not without its attractiveness.
It is theatrical, operatic. Perhaps it ought only to be seen
against the background of the Mass performed in a church
of that period when 'one sees no longer a mere world of
marble and paint, a human world, but a great composition
in which the movement of the painted figures and the
ritual of the priests combine in a grand symphony . . . an
accessible image of the beyond, an operatic spectacle.'[2]

The eighteenth and nineteenth centuries produced very
little religious art which was distinguished. The exception
was William Blake, poet, artist, and mystic whose powerful

[1] *On Art and Artists*, A. Huxley (Chatto & Windus), p. 230
[2] *A Concise History of Art*, G. Bazin (Thames & Hudson)

drawings reflected his inward vision of the reality behind the created order (fig. 16). 'I assert for My Self that I do not behold the outward creation. When the sun rises, do you not see a round disk of fire? Oh, no, no, I see an innumerable company of the Heavenly host crying, Holy, Holy, Holy is the Lord God Almighty.'

There was no shortage of religious subjects for the attention of the Pre-Raphaelites, although it is interesting that many of them concentrated on the domestic and moral rather than the fundamental events of the Passion: *Christ in the House of his Parents*, *The Girlhood of Mary Virgin*, and *The Return of the Dove to the Ark* are typical of their interest. Holman Hunt's *The Light of the World* may be a good allegory, but is not a great picture. Ruskin, in *Modern Painters*, attacked the mediocre Christian art of this period: 'The group calling themselves Evangelical ought no longer to render their religion an offence to the men of the world by associating it only with the most vulgar forms of art. It is not necessary that they should admit either music or painting into religious service; but if they admit either the one or the other, let it not be bad music nor bad painting: it is certainly in nowise more for Christ's honour that His praise should be sung discordantly or His miracles painted discreditably, than that His word should be preached ungrammatically.'

At the end of the nineteenth century it is to an artist whose subjects were rarely Biblical that we have to turn to see works of religious art, works which point a way out of the barren cul-de-sac of the 'merely human' portrayals of Christ. Van Gogh was an intensely religious person and after several attempts to express his religious faith through preaching and living among the poor, he found his vocation in painting, working with the same sense of service and love as he had shown as a preacher. His letters give some clues as to his feeling about this and how it affected his work: 'I want to paint men and women with that something of the Eternal which the halo used to symbolize and which we seek to give by the actual radiance and vibration of our colouring.' Writing of Rembrandt, though the phrases might be well applied to his own work, he spoke of 'that heart-broken tenderness, that glimpse of a superhuman infinite that seems so natural.' With this in mind, look at his *Portrait of an Old Peasant* painted in 1888 (fig. 17). There is no halo, but is there not something of the Eternal in this face? Van Gogh sees the face of Christ in this old peasant; he does not see simply a man, but 'Christ in every man.'

He is describing on canvas what the Russian novelist, Turgenev, expressed when he wrote of an encounter with Christ:

I saw myself in a dream, a youth, almost a boy, in a low-pitched wooden church. The slim wax candles gleamed, spots of red, before the old pictures of the saints. . . . All at once some man came up from behind and stood beside me. I did not turn towards him; but at once I felt that this man was Christ. Emotion, curiosity, awe overmastered me suddenly. I made an effort . . . and looked at my neighbour.

A face like everyone's, a face like all men's faces. The eyes looked a little upwards, quietly and intently. The lips closed but not compressed . . . the hands folded and still. And the clothes on him like everyone's.

'What sort of Christ is this?' I thought. 'Such an ordinary, ordinary man! It can't be.' And suddenly my heart sank, and I came to myself. Only then I realized that just such a face—a face like all men's faces—is the face of Christ.

Turgenev echoes the parable in which those who feed the hungry and clothe the naked minister to Christ. It is He who suffers in the needy and rejected, and when Christians serve others they do so 'not simply because they care about their fellowmen, still less because they want to see a tidy world. They do it because they see in the needy and suffering those for whom Christ died.'

Twentieth Century

No modern artist has felt this more acutely than Georges Rouault. His life and art were devoted to those who suffered in an evil world. When he first painted the prostitutes of Paris and the clowns of the touring circuses he was accused of being obsessed with ugliness and with the tawdry. Yet this was to misunderstand him completely. He saw a world of suffering which had to be accepted and he expressed in his work feelings of sacred horror at a humanity which was estranged from God, flesh without spirit, lust without love. It was the misery rather than the obscenity of sin which he depicted, and in his portraits of Christ there is a human radiance which shines through a flesh that bears all the wounds of mankind. Some of his fellow artists, Daumier and Lautrec for instance, showed man as tragic and absurd, and only that; Rouault went beyond the tragedy and absurdity of life, pointing the way to a Man who had accepted everything in the human condition, who had become truly involved with the suffering of mankind, and through his death had given us hope. 'My only ambition is to be able some day to paint a Christ so moving that those who see Him will be converted.'

The Passion of Christ

The paradox which faces anyone considering the
Christian claims about Jesus of Nazareth (and we have
already observed this at work in portraits of the Nativity),
lies in the tension between the divine and human elements
in the person of Christ. While the Byzantine artists could
picture the awe-inspiring Judge and Prince of Heaven,
later artists saw Christ as 'a man of sorrows and acquainted
with grief, with no form nor comeliness that we should
look upon him, nor beauty that we should desire him.'
This conflict affects especially the portrayal of the Crucifixion where the tension is seen at its most acute. Is the
figure on the Cross to be seen as Christ the King or Christ
the Slave, 'the ideal man of perfect beauty or the suffering
outcast dying the death of a mutilated felon, the High
Priest of the order of Melchizedek or the slaughtered
victim of human violence?'[1] This contrast can be clearly
observed if one compares a Byzantine Crucifixion with the
Isenheim altarpiece by Matthias Grünewald (fig. 12).
In a Byzantine painting Christ is shown triumphant over
death, almost untouched by suffering. He stands on the
Cross as on a victory dais, often robed and crowned. The
Virgin stands at the side, dignified and proud. This is not
a suffering man but a triumphant God. And this was one
way of expressing the essential truth about the Cross,
namely that Death does not have the last word; that the
Gospel story ends not on Good Friday but after Easter.

None of these statements could be made of the Grünewald which presents a scene of unrelieved suffering and
horror. Set against the great darkness that has descended,

[1] *The Listener*, 18 June, 1964

Christ's body is strung on the Cross as if on a taut bow, the arms pinioned from shoulder to wrist by the twisted cords of the muscles, the armpits cracking under the strain. The body is blotched with wounds from the scourging, blood and pus ooze out, the legs are green and gangrenous. The spongy feet are clenched tight in contrast to the clawing fingers, twisted in agony. The head hangs down on the breast, the mouth is distorted with exhaustion and pain. The Virgin swoons in the arms of John the Disciple, Mary Magdalene laments this cruel fate, and John the Baptist points to the Saviour 'who must grow while I diminish.' Blood from a lamb flows into a chalice. There are hints that there is some purpose in it all, but the dominating impression is of the sheer magnitude of human suffering. This frightful deed was the deed of a cruel race in a cruel world.

Grünewald had painted this altarpiece for the hermits of St. Antony at Isenheim and to their house came the victims of the plague, especially of the disease known as St. Antony's fire. This picture confronted the patient in his last agony, so that as he faced the final hours of his life in what must have seemed meaningless pain, he was made to realize that another man had suffered as he was suffering, a man who had cried out in *his* anguish: 'Is it nothing to you all ye that pass by? Behold, and see if there be any sorrow like unto my sorrow.' Here the plague-stricken might begin to see why the writer to the Hebrews could say that Christ 'tasted death, for Everyman.' 'This was the Christ of the Poor, a Christ who had become flesh in the likeness of the most wretched of those he had come to redeem, the ill-favoured and the indigent, all those in fact upon whose ugliness or poverty mankind wreaks its cowardly spite. This was also the most human of Christs—a Christ frail of flesh, forsaken by the Father until such time as no further torments were possible.'[1]

Both paintings therefore say something of profoundest importance about the Crucifixion—that God uses the suffering of the Cross for his triumphant purpose, and that this is the horror of what men can do to a man who comes to them in perfect love. Compare this with the *Crucifixion* of Raphael (fig. 13). It is humanist rather than Christian. We have lost both the gloom and the triumph. 'The mystery of Calvary has been transformed into a beautiful, balanced, beribboned, and harmonious incident in an ideal Italian landscape. It is superb as a work of art, but it is inadequate theology; for it is no longer so much a symbol of a transcendent saving event as a reconstruction of a beautiful incident in secular history.'[2] Now though the Crucifixion was an incident in history it can hardly be described as a beautiful incident—if one limits it to what happened on one afternoon in Jerusalem; it can only be called 'beautiful' in the light of what happened later. Yet here both the suffering and the triumph have been washed away—the mourners are calm and graceful, angels delicately catch the blood which issues from Christ's side, and the peaceful landscape is bathed in a subdued light. There is neither the Prince reigning from the Tree nor the Man tortured with suffering. Rather we have a good man, who through a miscarriage of justice, is using the opportunity to set a good example to all men. There is certainly some truth in the assertion that 'the perfection of Raphael was the beginning of the

---

[1] *Grünewald*, Husymans (Phaidon)   [2] Bridge, op. cit., p. 54

dullness that characterizes much sacred art and makes it empty and lacking in vitality.'[1]

We look now at three interpretations of the same event from our present century. Broadly speaking, contemporary artists have either presented Christ as more than a mere man—conveying either by the semi-abstract technique of Sutherland, or the stained-glass window effect of Rouault, a figure of special significance; or they have shown him as a man of our own society and age, as in Stanley Spencer's scenes from the Gospels set in his native village of Cookham. The gossipy women in bonnet and shawl in *The Sabbath Breakers* are, for Spencer, our modern Pharisees, self-righteous, eager to condemn; and in the *Baptism by John* Jesus is immersed in the Thames at Cookham, with people in bathing costumes around him. We are forced to see the events which are so often portrayed in the costumes of the first century as events which affect us now. 'A Christ who is not contemporary is not the Christ,' wrote Tillich, and we must not protect ourselves from the Real Christ by the myths of antiquity. And so when Spencer shows us his *Way to Calvary* (fig. 10), Christ carries his Cross through the modern village street; just as in his *Crucifixion* there can be seen houses, telephone wires and a curious crowd climbing the wall to watch the men in red brewers' hats nail a man to the Cross as if it were their daily work.

Graham Sutherland's *Crucifixion* (fig. 15), which can be seen in St. Matthew's Church, Northampton (along with Henry Moore's *Virgin and Child* (fig. 5)), is a version for the twentieth century of Grünewald's great work. Indeed

[1] *Christian Church Art*, McClinton (Macmillan, N.Y.), p. 84

D

this must have been a conscious influence in his preparation for this painting, and for his other less well known
studies of the same scene. There is not the detailed realism
of the Grünewald, though the tension created by the
curve of pinioned arms and legs is there; the bystanders
have been replaced by the harsh rectangles which emphasize the desolation of the sufferer; the emacited legs and
the cage of the ribs remind us in our day of the sufferers of
Belsen and Auschwitz, just as the earlier painting spoke
to the sufferers of the plague. For the genuinely contemporary representation of the Passion of Our Lord must
help us to see the suffering of mankind as it is today and
the power of love in such a situation.

Rouault's faith compelled him to attempt just this. In
his *Miserere* prints (fig. 14), he sees the Passion of Christ in
the context of the horrors of war. We move from Calvary
to Flanders and back again, realizing that Christ is crucified afresh by man's inhumanity to man. A mother holds
a child in her arms—this *could* be a Madonna, but the
inscription which Rouault has written underneath reads:
Bella matribus detesta—War, which all mothers hate. The
sword which pierced the heart of Mary is seen as the fear
and poignancy of all mothers threatened by the shadows
of war. In *Christ Mocked by the Soldiers* he shows us the
Prince of Peace contrasted with our power-drunk and
fear-ridden world; and though we can see that many of
these engravings have strong roots in the Byzantine
tradition, they are still essentially works of our time, con-
fronting us with the sorrow and pity of suffering. 'Being
a Christian in these hazardous times I can believe only
in Christ on the cross.'

3. Architecture

'If you are going to build a church
   you are going to create a thing which speaks.
   It will speak of meanings, and of values,
   and it will go on speaking.
   And if it speaks of the wrong values
   it will go on destroying.
There is a responsibility here.'[1]

IF YOU had the responsibility of building a church, what
would be the questions uppermost in your mind? Would
you be concerned most of all in providing a building that
'looked like a church'? And if so, how would you make
your church distinctive if it were to be built near other
modern buildings in the centre of a new town? You
might give it a spire, and as it is a modern church, the
spire could be of aluminium tubing. You could surmount
it with an illuminated cross, visible at night throughout
the town. And this done, of what meanings, of what
values would the building speak? You could, of course,
start from another point altogether by asking 'what is a
church for?' and more than that, what is *the* Church for?
What kind of a community is it? What is its main activity?
What is its relationship to the neighbourhood in which it
is set? Rudolf Schwarz, one of the pioneers of modern
church architecture asked himself these questions and
came to this conclusion: 'For the celebration of the Lord's
supper, a moderately large well-proportioned room is

[1] *Towards a Church Architecture*, ed. P. Hammond (Architectural Press),
p. 66

needed, in its centre a table and on the table a bowl of bread and a cup of wine. . . . That is all. Table, space and walls make up the simplest church. . . . There have been greater forms of church building than this one, but this is not the right time for them. We cannot continue on from where the last cathedrals left off. Instead we must enter into the simple things at the source of the Christian life. We must begin anew and our new beginning must be genuine.'[1]

Before we 'begin anew' and look in detail at the development of modern church architecture, we must look at the way in which Christian churches have been built in the past. This cannot, for reasons of space, be anything but a superficial survey of some of the main periods of church building and design, but just as in the history of painting we noticed how the beliefs of an age were reflected in its art, so also the climate of belief in the Renaissance, at the Reformation, and in other periods is to be seen in the forms and shapes of church buildings of those times. It might seem too obvious to note, were it not so often overlooked, that the design of churches will be determined to some extent by the practical requirements for worship and that the nature of that worship has in turn depended primarily on the theological and liturgical climate of the age. As the theology changes, so does the worship, and so do the church buildings.

For the first three centuries of its life, the worship of the Christian Church was essentially of a domestic nature. In the New Testament we can see the elements of primitive worship developing—many of the early Christians worshipped on occasions in both Temple and Synagogue as

[1] *Liturgy and Architecture*, P. Hammond (Barrie & Rockliff), p. 20

well as in 'the breaking of bread and the prayers' in one another's homes. As the former Jewish institutions lost their influence in the later generations (though the traditions of those two types of worship were preserved, liturgically, in altar and pulpit, sacrament and word), Christian worship would most often be celebrated in a private house of one of the wealthier members of the local church. In time the room in which services were held may have been decorated and specially furnished, but the only surviving church before the age of Constantine, at Dura-Europos, is in the form of a 'house-church.' The main room used for worship was rectangular in shape, with a table towards one end behind which the presiding minister sat with the elders.

The official recognition of Christianity by Constantine at the beginning of the fourth century heralded the building of large numbers of churches throughout the empire, many of them of considerable size and splendour, for they bore witness to the new status of Imperial Christianity. At this stage two types of church developed simultaneously, and although there are exceptions, the general trend was for the Basilican type to be found in the west, while in the east the Domical or Rotunda type was more common. From the Basilican plan, a simple rectangle with an apse, there grew the later elaborations of nave, chancel, transepts and towers which became the pattern of Gothic architecture until the Renaissance. It is worth noting that the basilica was originally, in Roman times, a civil building and there seems to have been no sense of incongruity in taking a secular form and adapting it for religious purposes.

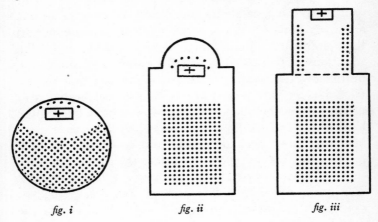

fig. i   *fig. ii*   *fig. iii*

In the earliest form of worship the arrangement of the congregation was very probably as in the first of these three figures; later the basilican shape compressed this into a more orderly form, though the same relationship of congregation and holy table was preserved (*fig. ii*). But with the addition of the chancel and the removal of the altar to the far end of it, the nature of this relationship changed radically and for the worse. The laity no longer gather round the table; they are not even within the 'choir' but are separated from the actions of the liturgy by a screen, beyond which the hierarchy of priest and deacons enact the mysteries (*fig. iii*). From the point of view of the congregation the altar becomes simply a visual image, a focus of attention, separated from its true function as the place of meeting for the family of God. Moreover, the larger churches of the early middle ages had much in common with the fortified castles of the period.

They have been described as 'palaces of God in which earthly knights of the heavenly courts defended their spiritual, intellectual and temporal properties, and with the distinction thought proper to that age between clergy and laity.' It was not until the Reformation that a doctrine of the church as the People of God, with its emphasis on the priesthood of all believers, was widely held, and this was expressed not only in Luther's writings and sermons but in the actual buildings which housed this 'family'. One of the immediate effects of the Reformation, therefore, was to remove the elaborate screen in many churches so that physical expression was given to these doctrines and the church became truly the house of the People of God. But although the screen might be removed and the altar brought forward to the chancel steps, the firm framework of the Gothic church remained and continues to dominate even twentieth century church building.

The Reformation had other effects on church buildings, especially in the Independent chapels and Quaker meeting houses that were produced by the Puritan and Nonconformist movement in England. Here a strictly functional interest dictated the shape and construction of the church. Since preaching was a prominent feature of worship, the pulpit became central; and so that congregations might hear easily, galleries were often built, with raked seats as in a lecture theatre. The communion table was placed in front of the pulpit to express the close unity between Word and Sacrament though in practice the celebration of Holy Communion has rarely been observed as the regular weekly worship of the non-episcopal Churches.

CHRISTIANITY AND THE ARTS

But this is not the only significant change in architectural history. For just as the Renaissance affected the portrayals of Christ in painting, so it affected the construction of churches. In the fifteenth century we see the beginning of circular, centrally planned churches. It is true that there had been the central churches of the early Byzantine period in the east, of which St. Sophia is an outstanding example, but these Renaissance buildings were of a different character. Liturgically they were ill fitted for the needs of the day—it was difficult to separate clergy and laity, the positioning of the altar was awkward, and so on. And it has been suggested that this change from Gothic to Renaissance reflects a change from 'other-worldly' to 'this worldly' concepts. 'The prime function of the medieval church had been to lead the faithful to the altar. In a completely centralized building no such movement is possible. The building has its full effect only when it is looked at from the one focal point. There the spectator must stand and, by standing there, he becomes himself 'the measure of all things.' Thus the religious meaning of the church is replaced by a human one. Man is in the church no longer pressing forward to reach a transcendental goal, but enjoying the beauty that surrounds him and the glorious sensation of being the centre of this beauty.'[1]

Just as Raphael was becoming interested in the perfection of form in his beautifully controlled portrait of a mother and her child (fig 3.) so Alberti was revelling in the perfection of number: 'I shall define Beauty to be harmony of all the parts in whatsoever subject it appears, fitted together with such proportion, and connection, that

[1] *Outline of European Architecture* N. Pevsner, (Penguin Jubilee Ed.), p. 295

nothing could be added, diminished, or altered.' Yet one must not dismiss Alberti's centrally planned church as necessarily leading the worshipper to glory in man, as Pevsner seems to imply. For Alberti contended that to contemplate such perfect Beauty is to contemplate God. Being convinced of the mathematical and harmonic structure of the universe, he argued that 'if a church had been built in accordance with essential mathematical harmonies, we react instinctively; an inner sense tells us, even without rational analysis, when the building we are in partakes of the vital force which lies behind all matter and binds the universe together. Without such sympathy between the microcosm of man and the macrocosm of God, prayer cannot be effective ... this architecture, with its strict geometry, the equipoise of its harmonic order, its formal serenity and above all with the sphere of the dome, echoed and at the same time revealed the perfection, omnipotence, truth and goodness of God.'[1] What had changed was the conception of the Godhead: Christ as the essence of perfection and harmony superseded him who had suffered on the Cross for humanity; the Pantocrator replaced the Man of Sorrows. Eventually the non-functional nature of the centrally planned church led to a fusion of the two plans, and many Baroque churches had centrally planned and domed east ends, with a nave attached. Wren's great model for St. Paul's Cathedral was for a central church, but the authorities insisted on the addition of a nave to his original plan.

With the Gothic revival of the nineteenth century it was not only the plan of the Gothic church which was

[1] *Architectural Principles*, R. Wittkower (Univ. of London, 1949), p. 27

copied. The design of the medieval craftsmen was slavishly imitated in the detailed decoration of the building and because of this it lacked any vital inspiration. Men like Pugin insisted that to build in the forms of the middle ages was a moral duty, and while the architecture of public buildings of that period reflected a number of styles, the majority of the churches were deliberate imitations of the medieval cathedral and parish church. This was not always the fault of the architect—there was pressure from the client to produce churches with this 'Gothic glow'. The romantic associations of a religion dominated by its past still linger on for many people, so that 'the smell of old damp stone or Victorian hassocks are a prerequisite of church furnishings, even of Christianity itself.' This is a serious state of affairs on two counts. First, a living art must work in the forms and media of contemporary society, and secondly, the medieval structure of the church expressed an implicit view of its function which is no longer accepted as either true or relevant. And although many 'modern' churches may appear to be expressing new techniques and materials in their construction, they may still be perpetuating, unconsciously perhaps, the Gothic image of the Church—Gothic in modern dress, as it were, a 'glossy paperback edition of the nineteenth century classics.'

It is from this standpoint that much rethinking of the nature of church architecture is now taking place; from an examination first of the function of the Church, and then of the ways in which architect and builder can provide for this function through their vision and skill.

Four factors have combined to give the present generation a unique opportunity for the building of churches:

1. The destruction which resulted from the last war
affecting thousands of churches on the continent and in
this country. Many have had to be rebuilt.

2. The growth of new towns and housing estates.

3. The development since the war of new techniques of
building and the use of new materials.

4. The theological revolution in thinking about the
purpose of the church and its worship.

These factors ought to guarantee that our new churches
would have an integrity and relevance about them.
Broadly speaking, while this may be true of many continental churches, the examples from Britain are very
disappointing, with a few exceptions. Of the twenty-
eight consecrated buildings in this country illustrated in
Sixty Post-War Churches, all but three are based on the
normal traditional church plan of the Victorian period,
with the altar at the far end of the chancel, separated from
the congregation by the choir, and sometimes a screen,
with pulpit and lectern standing at either side of the
chancel steps and the font at the west end of the church.
These buildings need not appear old-fashioned, for their
decoration is contemporary. Yet it has been pointed out
that nothing is easier or more irrelevant than to disguise
what is basically a nineteenth century building in contemporary fancy-dress. 'Merely having an odd look,
being the possessor of a Dreamland look-out tower,
having a glass wall that at a touch disappears beneath the
floor, displaying a mosaic of obscure symbolism constructed
of broken bottles, or exhibiting a statue by a name

guaranteed to strike terror in the conservative, does not constitute a new approach to church building.'[1]

Those who take this point of view regard with some misgivings buildings like Coventry Cathedral which are generally acclaimed as the outstanding achievements of modern church building. We shall discuss later whether the cathedral image is one which we ought to perpetuate, but Peter Hammond, for instance, has argued that Coventry 'is a building which contributes nothing to the solution of the real problem of church design and perpetuates a conception of a church which owes far more to the romantic movement than to the New Testament or authentic Christian tradition.' He goes on: 'The fundamental problem which we have to face today is one not of style but of *function*. It matters comparatively little whether the detail of a building is Gothic or contemporary; whether a church contains elegant Corinthian columns or parabolic arches of reinforced concrete; whether its windows are filled with insipid Victorian transparencies or with abstract patterns of glass slabs set in cement in the latest Paris fashion. What *does* matter is whether or not the building embodies a modern understanding of the Christian mystery; whether or not it is informed by a theological programme. . . . If it is not so informed, then no amount of contemporary detail, no glass or sculpture or painting, however fine in itself, can make that building a modern church.'[2] Hammond raises a fundamental point of debate about the nature of church building and not all would agree with him. Should we be concerned primarily with the visual effect of the building, both on the worshippers who enter it and those who

merely see it from the outside? Should we try to imitate
the great cathedral buildings of the middle ages and
thrust skeletal bell towers or illuminated crosses into the
sky as an affirmation of Faith? Is a church to be a place
for the corporate action in worship of the whole people—
'a machine for worshipping in,' or 'a sort of jewelled cave
in which the solitary individual may find some kind of
worship experience, and where his emotions may be
kindled by the contemplation of a remote spectacle'? Or
can it, perhaps, be both? These are questions worth discussing because they represent different attitudes to the
nature of Christianity and the purpose of the Church in
the second half of the twentieth century.

We can see the importance of a 'functional' approach
in architecture if we look at the way in which an architect
designs a school. It is unlikely that he will sit down and
think how he can best design a symbol of the nobility of
education and express this in his arrangement of buildings
and materials. He is more likely to design a building
which will serve a practical social function as a place of
education, in which the rooms and their relationships will
be dictated by what must happen in that building; how
the school must function. 'A good school building will
show us how society regards its children and what it
wants for their education; it will reflect the contemporary
understanding of education. But no school architect would
set out with the intention of making his building a direct
portrayal of some abstract theme or a means of arousing
in us the right feelings about education.' These sound
architectural principles seem to desert architects when they
are asked to design churches; or to be fair to them,
perhaps they are expected by their clients to construct

sculptural shrines of religious art rather than houses for the assembly of the people of God, or, as one architect described them more bluntly, 'liturgical sheds.'

What the architect needs to be given therefore when he designs a church is a 'liturgical brief' which sets out the essential relationships and actions of ministers and congregations in worship so that the positioning of font, altar and pulpit are not decided on purely visual grounds—will it look nice here or there; in red or blue?—but on the basis of the relationship between baptism and eucharist, between the Sacrament and the preaching of the Word. And he will also need to bear in mind the very nature of the Church itself, for one of the paradoxes in a discussion of church architecture is that church buildings are not strictly necessary for Christianity in the sense in which pagan shrines, or the Temple at Jerusalem were necessary to other faiths. For the Christian Church is essentially a community of people, and even to apply the word 'church' to a building is secondary and must remain secondary.

We have so far been thinking mainly in terms of the local church building, and most of the interesting examples of this at the moment are to be found in Europe (figs. 18, 20–23). In this country, however, we do boast a 'modern' *cathedral* which has been the centre of discussion and interest since the plans were first published. Some would raise the fundamental question as to whether we should build cathedrals in a post-Christian society and say that to attempt to recreate the grandeur, even in contemporary forms, of the Gothic cathedral is an expression of misguided nostalgia. The subject is controversial and it might be worth looking at contrasting views on the functions of the cathedral in, say, the thirteenth and twentieth centuries.

A critical view of the Gothic cathedral is that of an American Bishop who once described it as 'a rhetorical assertion of the temporal triumph of Christendom, a symbol of the domination of the world by the Church. It typified wealth and power and esteem, if not downright human pride. It chose mass and bulk and height as the necessary concomitants of its imaginative display; the greater the mass and the more exalted the height, the more impressive the symbolism, until, in the course of time, it encountered the humiliation of Beauvais. All this, however, had very little relation to actual use or useful-ness, for the cathedral, quite obviously, was not pri-marily designed to house the family of God. Moreover, the practical enslavement of the Christian world to the symbolism of the cathedral changed and warped the original concept of the Christian liturgy as the act of communal worship.'[1]

This criticism is not without its point and value. But it begs too many questions. Words like wealth, grandeur and pride must not make us forget that the Gothic cathedrals were built by people who believed absolutely and unquestioningly in God and were endeavouring to give expression to this faith by raising buildings at great personal cost and with money they could ill afford. The Gothic masons and stone carvers worked with a humility and anonymity unknown to modern artists, and much of their best work, which they took infinite care and pleasure in creating, may still be seen in roof bosses and carvings which were never intended to be visible to human eyes

[1] *Liturgical Arts*, Nov., 1958

but were offered solely for the glory and honour of God. The collapse, at Beauvais in 1284, of the choir vaulting, soaring to one hundred and fifty-seven feet above the floor, may be evidence of a failure of architectural technique, but the aim of the cathedral builders was to raise the mind to God by pushing the vault ever higher, building lighter and lighter with more and more glass, less and less wall, pointing a finger with soaring arch, flèche and steeple to where He reigned in the heavens.

The Gothic cathedral was a natural and spontaneous expression of a society sure in its faith. The cathedral of the twentieth century is in this sense something of an anachronism. The fragmentation of the faith, the divorce between religion and society, and the bankruptcy of religious symbolism pose peculiar problems to those who would design a modern cathedral. Of the four cathedrals built in England in this century, two of them, Liverpool and Guildford, are undisguised attempts to build in the Gothic style. The most unorthodox design is for the new Roman Catholic cathedral in Liverpool, which, with its centrally planned features, offers the most distinctive break with the Gothic tradition and attempts to rethink the function of the cathedral in contemporary society. The fourth, Coventry, is the one which has aroused most attention and since its consecration in 1962 has attracted millions of visitors.

It can be said at once that there are many fine things about Coventry. Viewed in the context of the rebuilt city centre it is as if the Church has its place with industry and commerce in the life of the community. The Chapels of Industry and Unity reflect the present concerns of Christians, and by its patronage of the arts it revives a

Fig. 2. Cefalù Cathedral: *Pantocrator*

Fig. 3. Raphael:
Madonna with Pomegranate

Fig. 4. Russian Ikon:
Madonna and Child

Fig. 5. Henry Moore: *Virgin and Child*

Fig. 6.   Graham Sutherland: *Christ enthroned*

Fig. 7. El Greco: *The Agony in the Garden*

Fig. 8. Giotto: *The Betrayal*

Fig. 9.
Rembrandt:
Christ at Emmaus

Fig. 10.
Stanley Spencer:
Christ carrying the Cross

Fig. 11. Michelangelo: *The Creation of Man*

Fig. 12. Grünewald: *The Isenheim Altarpiece*

Fig. 13. Raphael: *The Crucifixion*

Fig. 14.
Rouault: *Obedient unto Death*

Fig. 15. Graham Sutherland: *The Crucifixion*

Fig. 16. William Blake: *The Ancient of Days*

Fig. 17. Van Gogh: *Portrait of an Old Peasant*

Fig. 18. *Methodist Church, Upper Norwood, London*

Fig. 19. *Altar Cross (in silver)*

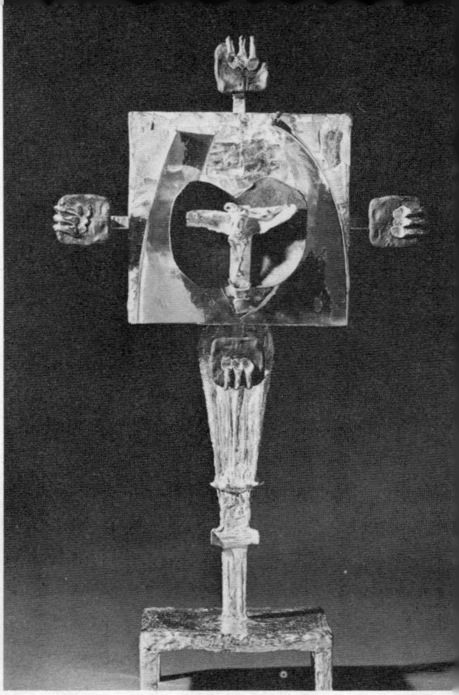

Fig. 20.
*St. Christophorus,
Köln-niehl*

Fig. 21. *Pilgrim Chapel, Ronchamp*

Fig. 22. *Pilgrim Chapel, Interior*

Fig. 23. *Coventry Cathedral, St. Michael and Satan*

link between Church and artist that is so often neglected. Indeed, so unusual is it nowadays for the Church to use the work of artists that there is a danger that visitors to the cathedral are apt to treat it as a religious museum or art gallery. The first question the visitor to Coventry may be asked is: What did you think of the tapestry? It is natural that we should want to see the Sutherland tapestry, the Piper window, the glass screen by John Hutton, the Lectern of Elizabeth Frink, the Epstein *St. Michael and Satan*. But these should not be viewed as isolated works of art, nor were they designed as such. Certainly they are not, as is too often the case, the after-thoughts of church furnishers, looking about for items to put into a bare building. They are part and parcel of a building erected to the glory of God and using the talents and vision of the artists.

It has been argued, however, that for all its modernity Coventry remains, in type, essentially a Gothic cathedral. Superficially it may appear to speak in the language of our age; basically it is a Gothic shell decorated by twentieth century artists. Critics like Peter Hammond and Gilbert Cope point out that what has dominated the architect's design is a romantic vision rather than a functional analysis of what kind of a building a cathedral needs to be. Its main function, they argue, should be liturgical: it is to house the people of God at their worship. On the same grounds that the neo-Gothic parish church has been criticized—for perpetuating the 'high' altar, the choir, and nave, so Coventry is attacked. It is true that there is no screen, nor are there transepts. Yet for many of the congregation the altar is remote, unsuitable for the primary act of the Christian family at worship, the Eucharist.

E

But Coventry cannot be dismissed as easily as this. It is clear that a central altar has some advantages, particularly when a large congregation is celebrating Holy Communion. But eucharistic worship is not the only, or even the main, liturgical function of a cathedral, as it may be in a parish church. The cathedral has many functions. It serves as a building in which different forms of services can be held which do not usually take place in the parish church, such as ordination services, diocesan gatherings or occasions when sacred music will be performed. For these conditions a centrally planned building is not functionally superior to, say, the Gothic plan.

But there is another 'function' of the cathedral, quite apart from that of providing a room for worship. It should glorify God, and the symbolism which is used must not be so mystical or remote that it does not make an impact on ordinary people. To judge from public reaction following its consecration, Coventry seems to have been very much a building 'for the people.' One symbolic danger of the centrally planned church is at least avoided. It is possible, though not necessary, for those who advocate the central altar and who talk in terms of a 'ritually initiated fellowship gathering in hierarchical order for the celebration of the Eucharist' to tend towards an introspective type of church, a community concentrating on its own piety and fellowship, and this may well be a bad thing. A. C. Bridge has pointed out that the Byzantine precedent for a centrally planned building arose in a period when the church was in progressive theological flight from the world. The world outside was a vale of tears, a lost realm, and the Christians looked to a city that was built in the heavens, ritually

enacting their drama of salvation amid the gilded walls
that shut out the mundane darkness. This is an under-
standable product of the period, but hardly one which
the church ought to wish to cultivate in the present age.
The modern church, with its involvement in unity,
industry, politics, and its exploration of new frontiers in
theology must be a community that is outward looking.
The Church is more than a Eucharistic fellowship. 'It is
the pilgrim people of God, a people called out of old
certainties and old securities, like Israel, to follow the
risen Christ wherever he may lead. And if Coventry is not
a triumphantly magnificent symbol of this, at least it is
a very good attempt to create such a symbol in an age
when it is particularly difficult to deploy Christian
symbols of any kind at all.'[1]

[1] *The Listener*, 6 Dec., 1962

4. Music

IT IS said of Schumann that he had just finished playing a new and as yet untitled composition to a friend who, puzzled by the piece, asked what it meant. 'It means this,' Schumann replied, and played it again. This incident illustrates the difficulty, if not the impossibility, of making any valid and helpful comparisons between music and the other arts. Music begins where words leave off, and the language of music can never be fully understood except in its own sounds and forms. We can try to compare it with the other arts but not without losing much. We could describe some music as 'architectural' where the structure of pure form is the most obvious characteristic, as, say, the music of Bach; we could also think of other music as 'pictorial,' in that the composer deliberately uses sounds to create visual images in the mind of the listener, as did Delius in *On Hearing the First Cuckoo in Spring*; and we could recognize affinities with literature when music is directed towards evoking and expressing human emotions. But these are only partial analogies and it might be better to accept Goethe's statement that 'in music the dignity of art reaches its fullness, because in it there are no material accessories from which in the end we should have to abstract. It is wholly form and content; it has the faculty of ennobling all that it expresses.' In this sense it is the most spiritual of all the arts and one especially fitted to the praise of God. 'The Church knew what the Psalmist knew: music praises God. Music is as well or better able to praise Him than the building of the church and all its decoration; it is the Church's greatest ornament.' So Stravinsky wrote and in the same passage criticized the tendency of the Church to view with suspicion music as 'antimoral.' In similar vein even the dour Scot, Thomas Carlyle, once wrote that 'music leads man to the edge of the Infinite and lets him for a moment peer therein.'

The Church was not the first to suggest that music could have a corrupting influence. Plato, in his *Republic*, had advocated education in music 'because more than anything else rhythm and harmony find their way to the inmost soul, and take the strongest hold upon it, bringing with them and imparting a right mind if one is rightly trained, and otherwise the contrary.' The Hebrew prophets had attacked those 'who sing idle songs to the sound of the harp and, like David, invent for themselves instruments of music' (Am. 6. 5). In the Early Church, which inherited the Jewish Psalter and added early Christian hymns, music properly formed part of the regular worship of the congregation, though again not without awareness of the dangers of using secular and pagan music which, through its frequently orgiastic associations, might be degrading. It was not until St. Augustine's *De Musica* that an adequate critique of music and theology was put forward. In this work Augustine speaks of music as an activity of the reason, not merely a matter of feeling and self-expression, and that which is 'bad' in music he sees as part of the heritage of imperfection in all creation.

It is impossible in the scope of this chapter to give a detailed survey of the history of Church music, but certain landmarks in the relationship between music and the Church can be mentioned. One important difference, in this respect, between music and the other arts is that music lags behind the visual arts which, for example, were already in a mature form by the time of the Reformation and could look back on a glorious past. Music, on the other hand, only achieved maturity in an age when the medieval synthesis had been shattered. There is no contemporary musical equivalent, that is, for Giotto, Dante or Chartres.

The Reformation and the emergence of polyphony were two factors which had a significant effect on the course and nature of church music. By the sixteenth century, the great polyphonic composers Lassus, Victoria, and Palestrina, were producing masterpieces for the Catholic churches of the Continent, though it is interesting to note that in mass and motet settings secular tunes and secular words were often used, until the Council of Trent prohibited this fusion of the sacred and secular. Under the influence of that Council, these composers were seeking to promote music which might in new ways teach men to feel 'that the House of God may be truly seen to be the House of Prayer.' At the same time the Reformers, with a new vision of the Church as composed of all God's people, were providing music written specifically for the people. In the Lutheran Church secular folk-songs were taken and 'baptized' for sacred purposes and the congregational 'chorale' became a staple ingredient in the reformed diet of worship. Calvin, with a more rigorous attitude to music acted on three principles: First, music is for the people, so it must be simple; secondly, music is for God, so it must be modest; and, thirdly, these objects are best attained by the music of the unaccompanied voice. The immediate result of Calvin's influence was the Genevan Psalter, with the simple yet sturdy musical settings of the metrical psalms, which developed later into the 'hymn.' This provision of new musical forms for use in church by the Reformers, together with the disciplines demanded of its composers by the Catholics, tended to set up a firmer dividing line between sacred and secular types of music.

If we are to seek for a parallel 'Renaissance' in music, we would have to place it about 1600 when the first opera was composed and when, for the first time, we have a solo voice, accompanied by instruments, singing an extended *aria*; tune becomes distinguishable from harmony, the solo from its accompaniment. 'The solo declamation was used not only so that words could be clearly heard, but so as to give free play to individual passionate utterance. In doing so, they brought into being a new conception of melody, modelled on the inflexions and rhythms of speech, seeking tension through augmented and diminished intervals and pathos through plaintive drooping phrases.'[1] The new music was not limited to vocal works and with the growth of purely instrumental music and the emergence of a set tonality, with major and minor keys, the nature and characteristics of orthodox European music for the next three hundred years were established. This music was neither sacred nor secular, except by association; it was rather a new absolute language, to be used or ignored by the Church.

The name of J. S. Bach is sufficient evidence that the new music could be used 'for the greater glory of God.'

[1] *Music and the European Mind*, W. Dunwell (Jenkins), p. 115

These were the words with which Bach countersigned most of his compositions—from 'secular' cantatas written at the command of his patron, to the *St. Matthew Passion*, written as part of his responsibility as the Kappelmeister at St. Thomas' Church, Leipzig. He used to perfection the influence and inheritance which were his. 'He was the only composer,' wrote Newman, 'who was able to use to the full, in practice, the theoretical possibilities of his art.' It is difficult for us to realize that the work of this one man, which foreshadowed the music of the next century, was hardly known in his own day outside the courts and churches for which he wrote as a composer-craftsman, faithfully undertaking his weekly obligation to provide church or court music for his employers. In his music Bach both relates and comments on the Gospel drama, and nowhere more movingly than in the *Passions* where evangelist, choir and congregation take part in a dramatic meditation on the meaning of the Crucifixion. In his *Mass in B minor* a new type of work is emerging— a work which has its origins in the liturgy but which was rarely to be performed as part of a church service. It eventually became music for the concert hall, to be performed for an audience rather than for a congregation.

This was but one of a succession of sacred works which have sought to express elements of the Christian faith in a musical form, but which are often presented before audiences containing many who do not accept the tenets of that faith. The concert repertoire of the large choral societies will almost certainly contain such works as the *Missa Solennis* of Beethoven, Handel's *Messiah*, Haydn's *Creation*, Brahms' *Requiem*, Elgar's *The Dream of Gerontius*, and, from more recent years, Walton's *Belshazzar's Feast*, and Britten's *War Requiem*. It is important to remember that until the nineteenth century, church music was always the music of the day. Music of previous generations was neglected and unknown to most people. Yet we know very little about the kind of music sung in local parish churches in, say, the seventeenth century. The composers who are remembered today—Palestrina, Byrd, Gibbons —were writing music for the Cathedrals and the Chapel Royal, not for musically inarticulate congregations.

The nineteenth century, which saw the emergence and flowering of romanticism, was a depressing period for music within the context of church life. Aware as we are of the danger of a preoccupation with the beautiful in art, the musical rhetoric of that century was particularly open to the dangers of an exploitation of the emotions. Music was sometimes used as a 'tool,' a means for producing a desired effect, evoking certain associations, and this is a legitimate aim for the composer of integrity. Bach had used chromatic harmony and discord in the *Passions* to heighten emotional tension, or to express anguish; Chopin used a driving rhythm in the *Polonaises* to arouse patriotic fervour; but the imitators of composers like Chopin and Liszt 'sought to achieve the pictorial effect of *Rustling Leaves* or any other similar subject of romantic imagery without any pretension to musical integrity, with the result that their music could not be, as that of Liszt was, a thing to be enjoyed and admired in itself, but could only be used as a means of conjuring up the "atmosphere" of spring-time in a well-sealed suburban drawing-room.'[1]

Extend this deplorable habit to the realm of Church music and we have 'hack music' being designed to convey

[1] *The Church and Music*, E. Routley (Duckworth), p. 178

and stimulate a sentimental religiosity. Bad theology was set to bad tunes. It is only fair to add that in the nineteenth century more than any other, it was easier for the unskilful craftsman to get away with such music. The amateur composer came into his own and, with a few exceptions, Victorian music was either tedious or vulgar, lacking tension and challenge, and substituting a self-centred sugary repose for the objective glories of the Christian faith. Whatever else it might be, Church music should never be dull or complacent, and Victorian music was often both. This is particularly evident in the music of the popular evangelism of the Sankey and Moody revival. It is interesting how often in such movements the emphasis is on judgement in the preaching and on peace in the singing. In American revivals the musical inspiration had often come from the negro spiritual and folk music. In England Sankey found no such ready-made folk music, other than the music hall tune, a tune of escape and sometimes of pretentiousness. Fifty years later, the music of the *Billy Graham Song Book* showed similar defects—'They exploit the musical platitude, the cliché of rhythm. Thus they express a power-mysticism, a bid for influence over a partly drugged mob. Their "heartiness" is a resurrection without passion; fictitious sentiment generated by quickly resolved discords in the harmony is substituted for the passion.'[1]

There is, of course, a danger that the musically sensitive person will appear to take a highbrow attitude to music which he finds inferior but which other people may enjoy, and it must also be remembered that some of the music which seems sentimental and commonplace to us

[1] *Church Music and Theology*, E. Routley (S.C.M.), pp. 73–74

now was accorded high praise a generation ago. W. H.
Auden warns us that our love of the arts can blur for us
the distinction between a concert-hall audience, which is
a community of persons with the same taste, but, as a
rule, many different beliefs, and a congregation, which is
a community of persons with the same faith but, as a rule,
many different tastes. When we see the appalling sentimentality and vulgarity of some of the items displayed in
the windows of shops that sell devotional objects, we may
well wish that the iconoclasts had won, but the fact
remains that many people find them helpful symbols of
their faith. So Church music must try to avoid the tempta-
tion to be, on the one hand, too 'conformed to the world'
in seeking public acclaim and approval; and on the other
hand, too highbrow in standing on its dignity. Jesus was
accused in his day of a disgusting lack of taste by the
Pharisees, and the common people heard him gladly.

What kind of music do the 'common people' of the
mid-twentieth century wish to hear and sing in church?
'When I hear a Beethoven Symphony, I don't feel anything. When I hear our kind of music I feel something
way down deep, like oatmeal.' The American girl's
verdict (quoted in *Life* magazine) on Beethoven and 'our
kind of music' has seemed to some to present a challenge
to the Church, and it has been argued that to use 'pop'
music in worship would attract young people to the
services. Since the Christian faith is meant to be seen
and expressed in contemporary terms, it should use the
musical vocabulary of the common people. Both of these
contentions are debatable, but what is certain is that since
the appearance of Geoffrey Beaumont's *Twentieth Century
Folk Mass* in 1956, the somewhat conventional world of

English church music has been disturbed, and that so far
as hymn books are concerned a more appropriate title
nowadays might be *Hymns Ancient and Modern and Pop*.

The Folk Mass is a setting of the words of the Eucharist
as celebrated in the Church of England, and has lines that
are easy to sing even if their musical content is somewhat
unexciting. There is much repetition and the most impressive section of the work, if heard with an orchestral
backing, is the setting of Psalm 150. There are hints of
improvisation from trumpet and clarinet, and some of the
effects associated with the 'big band' in jazz. Its musical
weakness is more quickly revealed when it is performed
without this support. The Twentieth Century Church
Light Music Group was formed soon after the publication
of the *Folk Mass* and has produced a number of hymn
tunes and short anthems in a similar style: *Chesterton*, set
to the words 'Lord, Thy word abideth,' had already
appeared in the Mass, and was later included in the
Baptist Hymn Book of 1962. Of the other composers in
the group, Malcolm Williamson is probably the most
accomplished, for he brings to the task his considerable
ability as an acknowledged composer.

Unfortunately, the word 'pop' is open to a good deal of
abuse and misunderstanding. 'Popular' music could be
music created and performed by the people, or it could
be the music which is enjoyed and listened to by large
sections of the population—seduced and bludgeoned by
an immense commercial industry bent on selling, then
saturating and finally discarding the latest 'hit.' Beaumont's main argument for writing church music in the
idiom of the people (though whether his music does in

fact use that idiom is another matter), is that in the apostolic days the music used at the Eucharist was 'the normal music of the day, and only became 'church music' when it arrived with definite church associations in Western Europe, where it developed itself into the plainsong we know.'

His main contention is not historically accurate in that it seems unlikely, from the evidence, that the early Church did use local popular music. But this need not detract from his hope that by providing his congregation with familiar music, the music they are accustomed to hear from their radios and record players, he helps them to see their worship of God set in the context of ordinary daily life. And that, just as one might feel that to read the lesson in the beautifully dignified rhythms of the Authorized Version might confuse and bewilder the congregation, so also to confront them with medieval plainsong or even Victorian chanting would have the same effect. Let the lessons be read in a modern translation, using occasionally a genuinely modern idiom or expression, and let the hymns be sung in the musical equivalent.

There are two points at issue here. One is concerned with the function of worship and the importance of traditional symbols. The other is whether in fact the music which Father Beaumont and others compose is genuinely 'pop' music, and if so, can it be held that this is the musical equivalent of, say, the New English Bible. Indeed, we cannot speak of a common musical language of our day, for there are at least four such languages: 'Pop' music of the Hit Parade; serious 'composed' music;

jazz; and popular 'light' music. One thing the Church
can do is to encourage these different languages rather
than favour some and condemn others.

Discussion of 'pop' Church music tends to be confused
because of its secular associations. Those who object that
it is unfitting to take the melody of a modern pop number
whose words may refer to love and sex, and use it as a
musical setting for a hymn, ought to be reminded that
one of the most hallowed of our Passiontide hymns,
O Sacred Head once wounded, started life, musically, as a
German love ballad, popularly 'crooned' in the middle
ages. And it is well known that many religious revivals
such as Methodism and the Salvation Army, seized the
contemporary popular music and brought it into the
service of the movement. 'Why should the Devil,' asked
William Booth, 'have all the best tunes?' Perhaps the
danger lies in treating (and judging) as a permanent
contribution to Church music, what should be essentially
an ephemeral one, possibly as transient with congregations
as on the sales charts. Very little of the modern Church
music in the 'pop' idiom has the staying power of, say,
the evergreen numbers of the twenties and thirties, or the
spontaneity of the negro jazz with which it is connected,
however remotely.

The irony is that both the music and lyrics of the
Twentieth Century Group seem hardly 'modern.' 'Banal
plushiness,' 'mighty Wurlitzer treatment,' 'moist-eyed
indulgences of parlour sing-songs,' are the verdict of one
critic. There is certainly a stale 'cinema organ' sound
about much of their work, while the lyrics are sometimes

taken from periods of hymn writing whose imagery would
seem to be the least intelligible for our age:

> His dying crimson like a robe
> Spreads o'er His body on the Tree. . . .

(set to slow rock tempo) or:

> Tread under foot our ghostly foe,
> That no pollution we may know. . . .

(from an old monastic hymn against fornication and set
to slow foxtrot rhythm).

If we are to seek to renew popular culture then we are
not likely to succeed if we take what is already a decadent,
if not deceased, form and then use it apparently to seek
popularity rather than artistic truth. An age *can* produce
its genuine folk-hymn, as did the Reformation and the
Methodist revival. The most fruitful sources in our
modern culture would be the field of genuine jazz, the
folk-blues spiritual, and the Shaker hymns, all of which
have their roots in protest—against slavery, exploitation
and the meaninglessness of the urban industrial environment. This, and their spontaneity, would seem to make
them more suitable for a Twentieth Century Church
Music Group.

One popular type of Church music has, however, won
wide acclaim and that is the psalmody of Fr. Joseph
Gelineau, a French Catholic priest who was dissatisfied
with the lack of congregational participation in the service
and who retranslated the words of the Psalter and set
them to music particularly suited to the verbal rhythm
of the words. There are several available recordings of
their use in congregational worship as well as by a soloist
with guitar accompaniment.

However misguided the 'pop' hymn movement may have been, it is at least to be welcomed for its desire to break down the barrier that had grown up in the last century between the musical conventions of the church and the world. Fortunately it is not the only sector of the musical world where this is happening, for the last generation is notable for the number of leading composers of international repute who have written music either for performance in church, or of specifically religious import. In this country, Vaughan-Williams was one of the leaders in the revival of the folk-hymn, as well as a composer of extended choral works, while Walton's savage setting of *Belshazzar's Feast* brought an unaccustomed sound to the Leeds audience when it was first performed in 1937. Stravinsky has welcomed the stimulation and opportunity that the Church offers for religious work, and Tippett, Britten and Maxwell Davies are among the more adventurous composers of music designed for small choirs in Church and for the concert hall. Davies' *O Magnum Mysterium* was written for the pupils of his grammar school and deals with the Christian mystery of the *Puer Natus*, the Boy and the Birth. Tippett's *A Child of our Time*, takes the theme of the innocent sufferer, and Britten both in the operas and in more explicitly religious works is dealing very often with childhood and innocence. 'We are obsessed with innocence because we have lost it; and because we have lost it, we persecute those who haven't. This is the theme that runs through much of his work *Peter Grimes*, *Billy Budd*, *The Turn of the Screw* are all concerned with the predicament of man and his loss innocence, while the *War Requiem* contrasting, as it does at one point, the voices of innocent children with the violence and horror of Owen's war poems, presents anew the Passion of Christ.

Continental composers have also written outstanding music in the Christian tradition. Kodaly's *Psalmus Hungaricus* and *Missa Brevis* have been described as two of the most impressive choral works of modern times, and his *Jesus and the Traders* is 'one of the most remarkable short works for unaccompanied choir of its age.' Quite distinct in style and interest is Messaien who has incorporated Hindu rhythms and bird-song into organ works which have elaborately theological and mystical titles, and which offer a new point of departure for that instrument.

It would seem, then, that in the twentieth century, church music has a chance of escaping from the barren cul-de-sac for which it seemed destined fifty years ago. Ours is an age in which both music and the Church are in something of an upheaval. The Church has lost the remoteness which made it able in other ages to turn at will a deaf ear to anything it considered 'profane,' and the ideas associated with the term 'religionless Christianity' have involved Christians in a living dialogue with the world. It is this conversation that must continue, and both the Church and music need their prophets who will no doubt be unpopular with some, as prophets usually are. But the radicals both in tonality and theology, and those of different musical and theological cultures and emphases must establish a 'creative counterpoint . . . for this will, in the end, determine the course that Church

F

music takes. There is at present no reason for supposing that that course will not take us through more exciting country, and more vital experience, than it has passed through up to now. All the signs are that it will, perilous though the journey will be from time to time.'[1]

[1] *Twentieth Century Church Music*, E. Routley (Jenkins), p. 213

5. Fiction

'HAVE YOU read any good books lately?' could be more than a conversational gambit if applied to the novel. For what constitutes a 'good novel'? We're not concerned at the moment with what might be called 'light literature,' the paper-back escape hatch into a fantasy world of adventure, crime, mystery, sex, love or outer space with which we try to while away a train journey. We are interested in those novels which speak seriously—though not necessarily without humour—about 'the human condition.' For this is the only proper subject of a novel, 'Man, the heart of man, and human life.' This human condition can never be conceived in abstraction, it is disclosed in and through vivid situations and in concrete images. The writer holds up a mirror to society, and through his understanding of human beings and their relationships he presents us with an image of man. The more able the writer and the deeper and more sensitive his understanding, the sharper the image will be. But the concern of the novelist will always be this exploration of the human predicament.

A Religious Novel

If this is so, is it possible to define a 'religious' or a 'Christian' novel? The pious reader asking a librarian for a 'nice religious book' for her weekly reading would be horrified if she were handed Graham Greene's *The Heart of the Matter*, with its seedy promiscuity in tropical Africa, or William Golding's *Lord of the Flies*, a nightmare of fear and murder on a desert island. These, it is true, are not 'nice books,' but they are religious books because they are both concerned with the problem of evil and the nature of man. *The Heart of the Matter* is the more explicitly Christian in that its central character, Scobie, is a Roman Catholic and his personal dilemma is described in the language of the Catholic scheme of salvation. In *Lord of the Flies*, the setting has no apparent connection with Christian symbols or vocabulary.

The Christian novelist, like other Christian artists, is faced with a problem. The dominant values of society are non-Christian: success in love or life is what matters most. Religion is relegated to a compartment of life, of rapidly decreasing importance, and religious language, for the majority of people, has lost its meaning. We seem not to need the old religious words. Charity, grace, redemption have become meaningless. In the minds of men today they belong to the childhood of the race, like the words 'fairy' and 'gnome.' Confident, prosperous modern man will, it is true, occasionally dispense charity; grace and redemption he thinks he does not need. This places the novelist in a difficult position if he wishes to write about specifically Christian themes. He could go back, in his writing, to a past age where his subject, Christianity, was not exceptional, immersing his readers in the thought forms of another period and through this identification presenting them with a religious interpretation or comment upon life. He could, on the other hand, choose for his novel a strange, almost bizarre setting, to emphasize the exceptional nature of his subject. Thus Graham Greene writes novels about revolutionary

Mexico, the underworld of Brighton, and a leper colony in Nigeria; or Evelyn Waugh portrays the brittle, sophisticated aristocracy of the twenties in *Brideshead Revisited*. A third way is to use myth and fable in the battle of good and evil as, for instance, in some of the writing of C. S. Lewis or Charles Williams.

Each of these ways has its limitations and it must not be assumed that novels need overt religious language or symbolism to make them religious. One of our Lord's most famous 'short stories' about the wayward son who became a rake before being restored to his family has very few 'religious' references. Perhaps the most effective way of communicating religious truth in fiction is to avoid taking a specifically religious subject. There is, of course, one danger in this, namely that the reader may be unaware of what the writer is trying to do. One can read such novels on two levels, so that to one person *Lord of the Flies* is an exciting, if at times gruesome, adventure of some school boys marooned on a desert island, while to another it is a fable of the Fall of Man and Original Sin. But then the same criticism was made of Jesus' parables —there are those, he said, who will hear these stories and not understand; will see the picture, but not perceive.

One way which is not open to the Christian novelist is to use his novel as a platform for propaganda or a vehicle for moralizing. It is tempting for Christians to do this, for they tend to be interested not so much in how and why people behave, as in how they ought to behave and what ought to be done about them. John Osborne, writing of his work, said that he was 'doing without the commercials.' He was, in other words, presenting life as he saw it, sometimes nasty, angry and sordid, and would let the situation

speak for itself, without the moral peroration at the end,
the plugs for good conduct, better living, etc., as the curtain falls. Indeed any novel or play which has to take
pause at the end and say, in effect, 'now the moral of all
this is . . .' has failed manifestly; whatever virtue or moral
there is should be so much a part of it, so built in, that
the work speaks for itself. And because the novel is about
life, it is about the whole of life, not just the pleasant parts
of it. Again, some Christians are too fond of looking at
life not as it is, but through the rose coloured spectacles
of sham piety. Such people like their novels to reflect a
pleasant utopian world, untroubled by dark and ugly
passions.

The genuinely serious novel cannot do this, for it is a
variation on the theme of disenchantment. Lionel Trilling
describes this enduring and suffering of disenchantment
as the *motif*, the essence of the art form as a novel. The
hero begins in a state of innocence; he undergoes tempta-
tion, he is seduced, deprived of his innocence, and from
this state of disenchantment he reaches upwards into
fulfilment—perhaps sadder and wiser, but certainly the
richer in his experience. Possibly one of the greatest
Christian novels is Dostoevsky's *The Brothers Karamazov*.
Ivan Karamazov is totally disillusioned—since God is no
more, everything is permitted, and his arguments against
the Church seem unanswerable. Yet the novel is Christian
because it holds up a mirror to the condition of men as
they are—Aloysha, Ivan, Dmitri—and in the end it is the
Christian insight which is vindicated.

Another considerable novelist of the earlier part of this
century, D. H. Lawrence, while not an orthodox Christian,
was certainly a religious writer. He saw with bitterness

what industrial life had done to human beings, and what a narrow puritanism had done to the human spirit. In his disillusion he looked to a God of creative sexual love who would deliver him from guilt, who would help him to fight the bitch-goddess success and throw off the restraints of an industrial society. He was disillusioned with the Christian Church which he felt had extinguished the vital flame of the God of Life, turning Him into 'an Insurance Policy interpretation of the Universe.' Despite some fundamental inconsistencies between his pantheism on the one hand and his presentation of a 'mighty, living God' on the other, at his greatest he can speak of the Christian-existentialist theme of engagement, of generous commitment to others:

Give, and it shall be given unto you
is still the truth about life.
But giving is not so easy.
It doesn't mean handing it out to some mean fool, or letting the living dead eat you up.
It means kindling the life-quality where it was not,
even if it's only in the whiteness of a washed pocket-handkerchief.[1]

And this commitment, this life-quality, is set in a context beyond the merely human:

It is not easy to fall out of the hands of the living God.
They are so large, and they cradle so much of a man.
It is a long time before a man can get himself away.
Even through the greatest blasphemies, the hands of the living God still continue to cradle him.[2]

These may appear oblique approaches to the nature of a 'Christian' novel and some people would argue that the

[1] *Collected Poems*, D. H. Lawrence (Heinemann), Vol. II, p. 178
[2] Ibid., Vol. III, p. 144

Christian writer should simply present a detailed account of what he imagines may have happened two thousand years ago—an historical novel of biblical times. The most popular recent treatment of the life and work of Jesus and the early Church have been books like Lloyd Douglas' *The Robe* and *The Big Fisherman*. Such a subject could be successful, though not many novels of this type have offered a particularly religious interpretation of life. It is not the devotion or sincerity of the author which is called in question but the overall effect of the books, interesting us in the life and times of the Roman imperial world rather than deepening our understanding of the Passion drama. Moreover, the historical method has one grave disadvantage. It transports the reader back into an earlier age so that the figure of Jesus is a figure of the past, and to some extent the more brilliant the reconstruction of the atmosphere of that age, the more removed we are from the essential Christ. For to the real believer Christ is his contemporary.

The Passion Drama

If a writer wishes to take a particular concept from the Gospel stories, then there are other ways in which it can be treated. An interesting study of this has been made by Dr. F. W. Dillistone in *The Novelist and the Passion Story*, in which he selects four novels and examines the various ways in which they have attempted to present this story in the setting of their own age. Mauriac in *The Lamb* gives us, in Xavier, a Christ-figure in terms of disinterested love; Melville in *Billy Budd* presents us with the innocence of the suffering Christ, the hero without malice and with childlike trust, innocent but condemned; in Kazantzakis'

Christ Recrucified, Manolios, wanting only to live in peace with the whole world, brings out the worst in the village Pope, and in the Judas-figure; and with his death we know that Christ is still crucified in the world and the struggle between good and evil never ceases; and in Faulkner's *A Fable*, we have an attempt, set in the 1914–18 war, to describe the fate of a figure who represents nothing more nor less than reconciling love in a world dominated by the twin gods of War and Mammon. 'And so,' he seems to be saying, 'if we of the twentieth century are to see the reality and meaning of the Passion, we must view it within the context of our own crisis, the crisis of total war with the world divided into two opposing halves, each assuming that its own salvation can only be gained through the complete annihilation of the other. For unless the Passion becomes real within the setting of war, war which destroys earth and home and decency and the rhythm of life and mutual respect and the intimacy of human relationships, it has no ultimate bearing upon the human situation.'[1]

Any of these novels could be read and discussed in some detail, with particular reference to Dr. Dillistone's thesis, and it is noticeable that despite some obvious and deliberate symbolism there is no attempt to represent the Passion of Christ directly, for to do this would be to invite failure. Especially with this aspect of the Christian faith, the paradox must be preserved. For there will always be the paradox, the tension, in the Passion drama between the heroic and the suffering Christ, the willing victim and the triumphant conqueror. In painting this raises particular problems, as we saw in Chapter 2, but in music and

[1] *The Novelist and the Passion Story*, F. W. Dillistone (Collins), p. 107

literature they are less acute. One reason why Bach's *St. Matthew Passion* is one of the supreme works of art is that it holds things in perfect balance. There is the savage cry of the crowd, 'Barabbas,' but there is also the victorious assurance of the final chorus, transforming the poignant horror of Calvary into a deep ground of man's hope. So too the novelist can, through his art, trace a man's course as in his own person the hero holds together Good and Evil, Freedom and Necessity, Heaven and Hell. There will never be a complete and satisfying resolution, just as there is no complete explanation and understanding of the Passion drama. But for all that, the attempt must be made. For the story of that drama tells us something about ultimate reality, it sheds light on the mystery of the human condition, and it points the way to reconciliation, that restoration of the broken relationships which estrange men from one another and from God.

Myth

If the Christian writer consciously takes the Passion drama as the inspiration for his work, there are other writers who would not acknowledge the Christian faith, but who find in the great myths of our culture a pattern for their work. 'Myth' is a misleading word since it often suggests imaginary and purely fictitious qualities. But in the ancient world 'myths' helped man to understand his experience and his environment. Nor did they only serve as an explanation of puzzling circumstances. As H. and H. A. Frankfort write in *Before Philosophy*:

> In telling a myth the ancients did not intend to provide entertainment. Neither did they seek, in a detached way, and without ulterior motives, for intelligible explanations of

the natural phenomena. They were recounting events in which they were involved to the extent of their very existence. They experienced, directly, a conflict of powers. . . . The images had already become traditional at the time when we meet them in art and literature, but originally they must have been seen in the revelation which the experience entailed. They are products of imagination, but they are not mere fantasy. It is essential that true myth be distinguished from legend, saga, fable and fairy tale. All these may retain elements of the myth. . . . But true myth presents its images and its imaginary actors, not with the playfulness of fantasy, but with a compelling authority. It perpetuates the revelation of a 'Thou.'

It is these myths—myths of the Fall of Man, of Hell or estrangement from God, of the Quest, the Voyage, of Sanctity, which are to be found deeply embedded in Biblical literature and Christian art, and which are still able to inspire the creative writer. They can be traced in Faulkner, Kafka, Camus, Mauriac and many others. But in the present chapter we shall confine our detailed inquiry to two English novelists.

Two Modern Novelists

William Golding

This concern with the nature of man, the problem of evil, and the existence of sanctity has dominated the writing of Golding and Greene. We look at their work in more detail partly for the practical reason that it is readily available in paper-back editions, and partly because each provides a fitting contrast to the other, Greene writing as a practising Roman Catholic Christian, Golding dealing on a larger canvas with the problem of Man.

Golding has written five novels since 1954 when his first work, *Lord of the Flies*, was published. He has also written a play, *The Brass Butterfly*, in which, at one point, Phanocles, an inventor, is talking to the emperor:

Phanocles: Caesar, I conquered the universe, and yet the ants have defeated me. What is wrong with man?
Caesar: Men. A steam ship, or anything powerful, in the hands of man, Phanocles, is like a sharp knife in the hands of a child. There is nothing wrong with the knife. There is nothing wrong with the steam ship. There is nothing wrong with man's intelligence. The trouble is his nature.

And so Golding explores the nature of man and creates in each novel a particularly enclosed situation so that man's essential nature is revealed and tested under pressure—a group of boys on a desert island; Neanderthal men facing the crisis of a new age and a strange people; the consciousness of a sailor drowning at sea; an artist looking back on his life from a prison camp during the war; the dean of a medieval cathedral obsessed with his desire to build a spire to the glory of God.

Lord of the Flies is set on a deserted tropical island. An atomic war has broken out and a plane carrying a party of schoolboy 'evacuees' has crashed. Only the boys survive and their immediate prospect is delighted anticipation of a desert island without grown-ups. With true public-school aplomb, they elect a leader, Ralph, and institute a council, summoned by a conch-shell. But gradually the restraints of society and the conventions of correct middle-class behaviour are forgotten. There are irrational fears—of the imaginary beast and the unknown darkness. The group splits up into the hunters who begin to revel in the blood-lust induced by pig-sticking, and those who try to retain their civilized standards and are despised by the hunters because they will not join them. Simon, Piggy and Ralph, all suffer at the hands of Jack and his hunters. The catching of a boar and the first taste of blood develop swiftly into ritual terror, almost uncontrollable in its violence. After the pig has been killed Robert starts to play with Jack, imitating the boar. The rest form a circle, moving round and beginning to chant.

The chant rose ritually, as at the last moment of a dance or a hunt. 'Kill the pig! Cut his throat! Kill the pig! Bash him in!'

Ralph too was fighting to get near, to get a handful of that brown, vulnerable flesh. The desire to squeeze and hurt was overmastering.

Jack's arm came down; the heaving circle cheered and made pig-dying noises. Then they lay quiet, panting, listening to Robert's frightened snivels. He wiped his face with a dirty arm, and made an effort to retrieve his status.

'Oh, my bum!'

He rubbed his rump ruefully. Jack rolled over.

'That was a good game.'

'Just a game,' said Ralph uneasily. 'I got jolly badly hurt at rugger once.'

'We ought to have a drum,' said Maurice, 'then we could do it properly.'

Ralph looked at him. 'How properly? . . .'

'You want a pig,' said Jack. 'You could get someone to dress up as a pig and then he could act—you know, pretend to knock me over and all that——'

'You want a real pig,' said Robert, still caressing his rump, 'because you've got to kill him.'

'Use a littlun,' said Jack, and everybody laughed.[1]

[1] *Lord of the Flies* (Penguin), p. 110

But it is uneasy laughter, and it is not 'a littlun,' one of the junior boys, who is the first victim, but Simon. Simon is Golding's saint, a character of genuine goodness, who sets out to climb the hill on which can be seen, swaying in the wind, an unnameable horror which strikes terror into the rest of the boys. Simon discovers that this 'beast' is actually the body of an airman, swaying in his para-chute, and hurries down to tell the others. But he joins them just when they are in the middle of a ritual dance, and they savage and kill him as he tries to shout his good news over their frenzied shrieks. From then, the hunt is really on. Piggy's glasses are stolen, and he is crushed to death by a rock catapulted from the hunters' stronghold as he makes his last protest, the protest of intelligence, reduced to impotent futility by the senseless behaviour of the mob.

The final terrifying hunt for Ralph is only ended by the unexpected arrival of a naval officer who had seen the smoke of the fire and come to investigate. He is puzzled by the dishevelled appearance of the boys who begin to gather on the beach.

'I should have thought,' said the officer, as he visualised the search before him, 'I should have thought that a pack of British boys—you're all British aren't you?—would have been able to put up a better show than that—I mean—'
'It was like that at first,' said Ralph, 'before things—' He stopped.
'We were together then—'
The officer nodded helpfully.
'I know. Jolly good show. Like the Coral Island.'
Ralph looked at him dumbly. For a moment he had a fleeting picture of the strange glamour that had once invested the beaches. But the island was scorched up like

dead wood—Simon was dead—and Jack had. . . . The tears
began to flow and sobs shook him. He gave himself up to
them now for the first time on the island; great shuddering
spasms of grief that seemed to wrench his whole body. His
voice rose under the black smoke before the burning wreck-
age of the island; and infected by that emotion, the other
little boys began to shake and sob too. And in the middle
of them, with filthy body, matted hair, and unwiped nose,
Ralph wept for the end of innocence, the darkness of man's
heart, and the fall through the air of the true, wise friend
called Piggy.

The officer, surrounded by these noises, was moved and
a little embarrassed. He turned away to give them time to
pull themselves together; and waited, allowing his eyes to
rest on the trim cruiser in the distance.[1]

The nightmare is over—but one is left uneasily wondering what is the true nature of man, when the veneer of
civilization, the trim cruiser in the distance, has been
removed. It is no coincidence that the officer quotes
Coral Island in those closing sentences; Ballantyne's book
is mentioned early in the novel as well, and there is more
than a superficial link. Golding has told us that he was
influenced by the work with its Victorian idealism and
complacency about Man. It was written in 1858 and
belongs to that period 'when boys were sent out of
Arnoldian schools certified free of Original Sin.' On
Ballantyne's Coral Island the three Britons, Ralph, Jack
and Peterkin, acquit themselves like honourable British
gentlemen, regenerate empire-building boys, spreading a
civilizing influence around, overcoming cannibalism, and
turning paradise into a British protectorate. But Golding
is doing more than reversing the situation in *Coral Island*—
here is a 'bedrock exploration of human nature.' At first,

Ibid., p. 192

every prospect pleases on this island too, but the vileness proceeds not from cannibals but from the boys, from within themselves. As the Beast, in conversation with Simon, says, 'Fancy thinking the Beast was something you could hunt and kill! You knew, didn't you? I'm part of you.' It is man who creates his own hell, his own devils; the evil is in *him*. And when Simon, having discovered the truth, tries to tell the others of it and is killed even as he speaks, it is as if Golding is saying that 'man cherishes his guilt, his fears, his taboos, and will crucify any saint or redeemer who offers to relieve him of his burden by telling the simple truth. Man's heart is dark and no innocence lives beneath the sun; or if it does, it must inevitably suffer and die as Piggy and Simon died, their wisdom and virtue destroyed by the Beast's devotees.'[1]

In *The Inheritors*, his second novel, Golding is still concerned with the fall of Man, and again there is a reaction against a book read in his youth, H. G. Wells' *Outline of History*. 'My father,' wrote Golding, 'was a rationalist, and the *Outline* was something he took neat. It is the rationalist gospel in excelsis. . . . But it seemed to me too neat, too slick. And when I re-read it as an adult, I came across his picture of Neanderthal man, our immediate predecessors, as being these gross brutal creatures who were possibly the basis of the mythological bad man. . . . I thought to myself that this is just absurd. . . .' Wells regarded the success of the high-foreheaded, weapon-bearing, carnivorous *homo sapiens* as progress, but to Golding it was the defeat of innocence, the sin of Adam seen in terms of a new kind of history. It is these new men who introduce guilt, crime and suffering into the world, and

[1] *Review of English Literature*, P. Green, April 1960, p. 66

when they triumph, Lok, the Neanderthaler, weeps as Ralph wept for the corruption and the end of innocence.

In his first two novels Golding is interpreting, in these very different situations, the myths which stand at the beginning of Genesis telling of the Fall of Man and Original Sin. In his third novel, *Pincher Martin*, he moves to the New Testament, from the problem of evil in mankind to the drama of the salvation or the perdition of an individual soul.

Pincher Martin is a naval officer during the war. He is on the bridge of his ship when it is torpedoed and he is flung into the sea.

> He was struggling in every direction, he was the centre of the writhing and kicking knot of his own body. There was no up or down, no light and no air. He felt his mouth open of itself and the shrieked word burst out.
> 'Help!'
> When the air had gone with the shriek, water came in to fill its place—burning water, hard in the throat and mouth as stones that hurt. . . . The lumps of hard water jerked in the gullet, the lips came together and parted, the tongue arched, the brain lit a neon track.[1]

These are the opening words of the novel and give some indication of the descriptive power which is sustained throughout the book as Martin's body is buffeted by the sea. Martin apparently manages to kick off his heavy sea-boots and inflate his lifebelt and is carried by the waves to a spur of rock which is battered by the waves. There he clings, and the main section of the book alternates between descriptions of 'life' on that rock—the water, the clothing, the texture and colour of the rock, the struggle for survival,

[1] *Pincher Martin* (Penguin), p. 5

G

and flash-backs into Martin's earlier life as the play-boy actor, ruthlessly selfish, hideously greedy—'he takes the best part, the best seat, the most money. . . . He was born with his mouth open and both hands out to grab.' 'Pincher' is not merely his naval nickname, it is an exact reflection of his personality, for he is greed and egotism personified. And the name he really bears, which is on his identity disc, 'Christopher,' the Christ-bearer, has been erased in this fallen man. So the ordeal on the rock continues until 'the centre,' the intelligence of Martin, disintegrates, shattered by 'the black lightning'.

> The lightning crept in. The centre was unaware of anything but the claws and the threat. It focused its awareness on the crumbled serrations and the blazing red. The lightning came forward. Some of the lines pointed to the centre, waiting for the moment when they could pierce it. Others lay against the claws, playing over them, prying for a weakness, wearing them away in a compassion that was timeless and without mercy.[1]

This might be the end of the story and the reader could be forgiven for imagining that what has been most brilliantly described has been the dying agony of a drowning man, soaked and battered by the sea. But there is a final chapter, a surprise ending. At a jetty in Scotland, a man has found Martin's body washed ashore; an officer arrives to collect it, and says to the fisherman, 'If you're worried about Martin—whether he suffered or not . . . then don't worry about him. You saw the body. He didn't even have time to kick off his seaboots.' So the book ends, and we realize that this is the author's way of telling us that the struggle on the rock didn't 'really happen.' It was

[1] Ibid., p. 184

undergone in Martin's mind within a few seconds as he died, catapulted from the bridge of the torpedoed ship, with no time even to kick off his seaboots.

When the novel first appeared some critics hailed it as a brilliant description of an heroic struggle for survival, and objected to the 'trick ending.' But when the work was published in America it was re-titled: *The Two Deaths of Christopher Martin*, presumably to avoid any ambiguity, and Golding himself has given us his interpretation of it: 'Christopher Hadley Martin had no belief in anything but the importance of his own life, no God. Because he was created in the image of God he had a freedom of choice which he used to centre the world on himself. He did not believe in purgatory and therefore when he died it was not presented to him in overtly theological terms. The greed for life which had been the mainspring of his nature forced him to refuse the selfless act of dying. He continued to exist separately in a world composed of his own murderous nature. His drowned body lies rolling in the Atlantic but the ravenous ego invents a rock for him to endure on. It is the memory of an aching tooth. Ostensibly and rationally he is a survivor from a torpedoed destroyer; but deep down he knows the truth. He is not fighting for bodily survival but for his continuing identity in face of what will smash it and sweep it away—the black lightning, the compassion of God. For Christopher, the Christ-bearer, has become Pincher Martin who is little but greed. Just to be Pincher is purgatory; to be Pincher for eternity is hell.'

As Simon is the saint in *Lord of the Flies*, so Nathaniel, a friend of Martin's from the old days, later serving on the same ship, is the saint in this novel. It is true he is a

shadowy character but his natural goodness is something
Martin recognizes and resents. At one point the two men
are talking of Martin's beliefs and Nathaniel says:

> 'Take us as we are now and heaven would be sheer
> negation. Without form and void. You see? A sort of
> black lightning destroying everything we call life.'

and a little later he adds:

> 'I think you need my lecture. You're not happy are you?'
> 'I'm not really interested in heaven either. Let me get
> you a drink.'
> 'No, thanks.'
> 'And I'm going to have a damned long life and get what
> I'm after.'
> 'And that is——?'
> 'Various things.'
> 'But you're not happy.'
> 'Why do you spill this over me, of all people?'
> 'There's a connexion between us,' replied Nat. 'Some-
> thing will happen to us or perhaps we were meant to work
> together. You have an extraordinary capacity to endure.'
> 'To what end?'
> 'To achieve heaven.'
> 'Negation?'
> 'The technique of dying into heaven.'
> 'No thanks. Be your age, Nat.'[1]

Dying into heaven is, for Nathaniel, being stripped of
our bodies, our contacts with physical reality, our relationships with others, and when this is taken from us we should
be nothing, a negation, unless another spiritual form has
developed in us based on service, humility, and love. The
experience of Martin, battered on the rock of his own
creating, is that he is slowly stripped of his relationships
with the physical world, and he is being invited to take

[1] Ibid., p. 64

on a new spiritual form. But this he resists—his egotism makes the supreme struggle for survival, he wants to be 'what I always was.' And so the black lightning of God's compassion eats away the periphery of his greed, until all that is left is the centre, and that too is greed, so Pincher Martin is destroyed.

This novel will shock those who believe that no soul will be destroyed, that no man can be so consumed by evil that he ceases to have a spark to respond to God's love, so that all, in the end, will be saved. But there is much in Christian teaching that supports Golding's thesis. His last two novels, *Free Fall* and *The Spire*, confirm his position as one of the most powerful and imaginative post-war novelists in England, and as one of the most religious. In these later works he continues to explore the nature of man and the very titles indicate something of his concern: Man's will is free, yet the Fall is a reality—self-destruction is a matter of choice; and the spire (which is added to a medieval cathedral) can be either a symbol of prayer to God, or the expression of a man's overweening pride. Only in this last novel is the situation obviously linked with generally recognized religious terms and situations, yet in all his work Golding is deeply concerned with the nature of man and his salvation.

Graham Greene

With Graham Greene we enter a different world. His literary style is far removed from that of Golding. He is influenced by the social-realism of the twenties and thirties, writing with that taut economy of words and an ease of narrative that immediately convey atmosphere. Many of his novels he describes as 'entertainments' and they have provided excellent material for the film producer. He is not concerned with myth and fable, as Golding is, though he *is* concerned with the sinful nature of man and the possibility of his redemption and, indeed, his damnation. His hero is the little man, the lost man, in a mackintosh; lowly, depraved, broken down. The setting is sordid: the sweat of the tropics, a gangster underworld, a grey industrial city, a seedy South American port. 'I stink, therefore I am.' Father Orfe's emendation of Descartes in Nigel Dennis' *Cards of Identity* seems to be aimed at Greene's 'Whisky Priest' figure of *The Power and the Glory* and *The Potting Shed*. 'An ascetic who is a heavy drinker and has fixed his point of self-recognition precisely mid-way between religious faith and the hip-flask.' In so many respects the world has turned sour—there is a terror of life, of what experience can do to an individual, of bitterness and corruption. 'Life being what it is, one dreams of revenge.'

Revenge dominates much of the action in *Brighton Rock*. The young Pinkie, seventeen-year-old Catholic and leader of a gang offering protection to bookmakers on the race-course, has become involved in a murder. Rose, a waitress in a café, is the only witness who threatens his alibi. To silence her, Pinkie decides, much against his inclination, to marry her. Rose is also a Catholic, and they decide to get married in a registry office so that the wedding will have no validity for them though it is sufficiently legal to keep Rose out of the witness box.

'Only marriage,' he said, 'will do for me. We got to be married properly.'

'We won't be that whatever we do. The father up at St. John's, he says.'

'You don't want to listen too much to priests,' he said. 'They don't know the world like I do. Ideas change—the world moves on. . . .' His words stumbled before her carved devotion. That face said as clearly as words that ideas never changed, the world never moved: it lay there always, the ravaged and disputed territory between two eternities. They faced each other as it were from opposing territories, but like troops at Christmastime they fraternized.[1]

This ravaged and disputed territory between two eternities is the essence of Greene's vision. The marriage of Rose and Pinkie is Blake's marriage of Heaven and Hell. 'Pinkie trailed the clouds of his own glory after him: hell lay about him in his infancy.' 'Credo in unum Satanum' was Pinkie's creed. Alone in his destructive world, he kills and he hates, hates even the love and hope which Rose feebly tries to offer him. In the end he is caught. Pinkie is tracked down by Ida Arnold, a woman determined to avenge the death of his first victim, determined to see Right triumph over Wrong. And with Pinkie's death it might seem that Right had triumphed. But there was a deeper level than right and wrong. In a conversation between Rose and Ida, Ida had said:

'I know one thing you don't. I know the difference between Right and Wrong. They didn't teach you THAT at school.' Rose didn't answer; the woman was quite right; the two words meant nothing to her. Their taste was extinguished by stronger foods—Good and Evil. The woman could tell her nothing she didn't know about these —she knew by tests as clear as mathematics that Pinkie was evil—what did it matter in that case whether he was right or wrong?[2]

And it is evil which triumphs over good. Pinkie's only legacy to Rose was a recorded message he had made on

[1] *Brighton Rock* (Penguin), p. 141 [2] Ibid., p. 201

Brighton Pier as a token of affection. After his death, when Rose first played it, she heard his voice: 'God damn you, you little bitch, why can't you go back home for ever and let me be?' This is hell's last word to heaven: 'Let us alone: what have we to do with thee? Art thou come to destroy us?' (Mk. 1. 24).

This battle between hell and heaven is fought out under different guises in the other novels. In *The Power and the Glory* the setting is a revolutionary Mexican state, ruled by a police force which is determined to rid the country of a superstitious religion, in order to establish a socialist progressive secular state. The central character is the only practising priest left in the country, hunted from village to village, with the problem of getting wine for his Mass and brandy for his courage. One can hardly call him a hero for there is little that is heroic about him. He is a failure as a priest, he has little ability, integrity, or moral courage. He feels himself abandoned in an abandoned world. And he represents, in his person, the Church. A Church stripped not only of its material qualities, for buildings, altar, vestments, even the missal are all lost or destroyed; but stripped also of its spiritual life and moral virtues—for courage, temperance, chastity, these too are lost. How can this be 'the power and the glory'? Towards the end of the novel, having crossed the border to safety, he returns to minister to a dying gangster. He is bound to this world with a bond of charity. This is literally his 'redeeming virtue.' On a night spent in an overcrowded common cell he realizes that

> This place was very like the world: overcrowded with lust and crime and unhappy love: it stank to heaven: but he realized that after all it was possible to find peace there,

when you knew for certain that the time was short. He was moved by an enormous and irrational affection for the inhabitants of the prison. A phrase came to him: 'God so loved the world.'[1]

So his faith and charity bring him to martyrdom. He does not die in a blaze of faith, but wretchedly, smelling of the brandy which has failed to drown his fear. And on the night of his death, a stranger lands at Tabasco, another exiled priest. So the work of the Church continues—a church stripped of every pretence and disguise, thrown back upon the love of God.

In *The Heart of the Matter* the location moves to the west coast of Africa. The hero, Scobie, is more attractive than Pinkie and the Whisky Priest of the earlier books. Indeed he arouses our pity, for he is caught in a web from which there is no escape, and it is a web created by his own compassion and sympathy. Again, the terms Right and Wrong do not cover the same territory as Good and Evil. Greene seems fond of choosing as the predilections of his characters what many church people might condemn as wrong. There is never any shortage of resolutions in church assemblies condemning drunkenness, violence, promiscuity and adultery. Yet Pinkie is violent, the priest a tippler, and Scobie, the police officer, tied to a wife he finds it difficult to love, has an affair with another woman. Faith and love drive him relentlessly on. His pity and love prevent his renouncing either his wife or his mistress; yet his faith dictates that he cannot continue to live in mortal sin and take communion. Since he wishes to

[1] *The Power and the Glory* (Penguin), pp. 125 and 127

protect his wife from the knowledge of his unfaithfulness he goes to Mass with her, and chooses damnation:

> He rose and followed her and knelt by her side like a spy in a foreign land who has been taught the customs and to speak the language like a native. Only a miracle can save me now, Scobie told himself, watching Father Rank at the altar opening the tabernacle, but God would never work a miracle to save Himself . . . with open mouth he made one last attempt at prayer, 'Oh God, I offer up my damnation to you. Take it. Use it for them,' and was aware of the pale papery taste of his eternal sentence on the tongue.[1]

This mortal sin is dramatically re-enforced with Scobie's suicide, carefully but not entirely successfully disguised from his wife. In the eyes of the Church, this is the last unforgivable sin, but the priest's closing words suggest that God's mercy is inscrutable: 'It may seem an odd thing to say—when a man's as wrong as he was—but I think, from what I saw of him, that he really loved God.' The heart of the matter is the innate sinfulness of man and his need for divine mercy.

Martin Jarrett-Kerr suggests that Greene's writing is too obviously conditioned by his temperament and faith. 'There is only one hero in every one of Mr. Greene's novels: a vague creature called Grace. His tawdry characters and stale scenery are evidently put there in a deliberately difficult obstacle race which the hero, Grace, is to run—high jumps made specially high to show his paces.'[2]

There is an obsession not only with pity, 'the terrible promiscuous passion which so few experience,' but with evil, and there is a tendency for his characters to talk not

---

[1] *The Heart of the Matter* (Penguin), pp. 216–217
[2] *Studies in Literature and Belief*, M. Jarrett-Kerr (Barrie & Rockliff), p. 164

to each other but to the audience, as if expounding for the reader's benefit an apologia for the Faith. It could be argued that his theological concern for the Catholic individual in his novels results in the literary weakness that the author 'is never really interested in more than one of his characters, and the rest stand, with their artificially invented unsupernatural lives, as a very cardboard-looking back-set for the drama he is trying to put on the stage.'[1]

Nevertheless, in their different ways, the one elemental, the other more schematized, Golding and Greene express a concern for the human condition. Their novels range over topics which the theologian would define as salvation, sin, hell, and justice. Their characters do not often possess the qualities which would earn them good references or election to the Church Council. But their books, along with those of Joyce, Faulkner, Cary, Mauriac, and others, are religious books. For 'a religious book is the result of a religious attitude to life. It is the product of deep compassion, of a fundamental seriousness about the reality of good and evil, about the depth and power of evil. It is a book that takes seriously the human predicament, that does not gloss over what is ugly and malign and misshapen. It is informed and suffused with a great pity for man in his plight. It sees man, not men; the individual in his solitariness, not types or stock characters. It may not use religious terminology or quote the words of Jesus, but it stands where He stood, for all that is living, spontaneous and free, against all that is dead, mechanical and necessitated. A religious book, no matter how sordid its characters or how foul its language, is a prayer of wrath and a plea for pity.'[2]

[1] Ibid., p. 166   [2] *Five Minutes to Twelve*, W. B. J. Martin (Collins), p. 123

6. Poetry

WHEN WE experience something unusual, either of pain
or joy, sorrow or love, most of us find it difficult to express
this except in hackneyed phrases or overworked adjectives
and clichés. We may describe a piece of music as 'fabu-
lous,' falling in love as 'terrific,' the view from a mountain,
'fantastic.' And if we have ever tried to express, in prose
or verse, the emotions and insights of such experiences we
immediately realize the difficulty of finding the right
phrases and cadences to make our experience come alive
for others. The poet's craft and genius lie in his use of
words, the patterns and rhythms which he creates with
them, the vision he communicates and the responses
which his work evokes in us. Like all artists he has this
twofold function of 'seer' and 'maker'—to perceive the
nature, beauty, and order of things and experiences; and
to create a form for this vision, to manipulate words and
images in order to describe and communicate it.

How does the poet, for instance, describe the agony of a boy
who watches his father slowly dying, passively, with resigna-
tion? Read Dylan Thomas' poem—or better still, hear the
poet himself read it—*Do not go gentle into that good night*:

> Do not go gentle into that good night,
> Old age should burn and rave at close of day;
> Rage, rage, against the dying of the light.
>
> Though wise men at their end know dark is right,
> Because their words have forked no lightning they
> Do not go gentle into that good night.

Good men, the last wave by, crying how bright
Their frail deeds might have danced in a green bay,
Rage, rage against the dying of the light.

Wild men who caught and sang the sun in flight,
And learn, too late, they grieved it on its way,
Do not go gentle into that good night.

Grave men, near death, who see with blinding sight
Blind eyes could blaze like meteors and be gay,
Rage, rage against the dying of the light.

And you, my father, there on the sad height,
Curse, bless, me now with your fierce tears, I pray.
Do not go gentle into that good night.
Rage, rage against the dying of the light.

If we try to analyse the way in which this poem achieves
its effect we have to talk about the rhythm and cadence
of the verse, the subtle and emotive power of words and
images 'charged with meaning.' Moreover, in this poem
in particular, there is an added experience gained when
the words are heard as sounds, and not merely read from
the printed page. The interaction and fine complexity of
all this fuses together in the poem and creates a unique
experience. Whatever it is we know in this poem, we
know only *in* the poem. Try to express this in another
way, in prose for example, and the experience will be
different. There is, in other words, a harmony of form
and content which is the essence of poetry. Something is
lost if, instead of, 'A thing of beauty is a joy for ever,' we
write: 'A beautiful thing brings everlasting joy.' For
'poetry should never be thought of as a versification of
prose ideas. Poetry is itself an instrument of discovery, a
means of exploration of truth and human experience. It

provides a way of penetrating into our own hearts and minds, of discovering in experience depths and subtleties that would never otherwise be apparent to us. It is a way of becoming more observant, more sensitive, more aware of the moving patterns and relationships in and behind experience. It is an activity that has its own intense discipline in which the choice of words leads to a sharpened awareness of the experiences the words are to express.'[1]

There have been many definitions of poetry. Matthew Arnold claimed that 'poetry is at bottom a criticism of life,' which provoked Eliot's apt comment: 'He might just as well have said that Christian worship is at bottom a criticism of the Trinity.' Others have described poetry as 'the language of the imagination and the passions,' 'emotion put into measure,' 'the best words in the best order,' 'perfection of form united with a significance of feeling,' or 'the use of language in such a way as to convey awareness of the imaginative wholeness of objects or their imagined unity.'[2] Certainly we may say that the poet, by exploiting the full possibilities of language, invites us to apprehend familiar objects, thoughts, events, and feelings, in a new and striking way, and to trace out imaginatively presented resemblances which deepen and enrich our experience of the world. To achieve this there must occur in the poet's use of language 'that perpetual slight alteration of language, words perpetually juxtaposed in new and sudden combinations.'

Because of this 'imaginative wholeness' which is the source of the poet's vision, there is a distinct affinity between poetry and religion, for both religious and poetic

[1] *The Creative Imagination*, K. Barnes (Allen & Unwin)
[2] Respectively: Hazlitt, Hardy, Coleridge, Eliot, D. G. James.

experience are concerned with a heightened awareness
and a sense of unity, and an attempt to find perfect
expression for these qualities. This is not, of course, to
say that religious verse is synonymous with poetry—indeed,
much religious verse is bad poetry. T. S. Eliot pointed
out that this was often because of a pious insincerity:
'The capacity for writing poetry is rare; the capacity
for religious emotion of the first intensity is rare; and it is
to be expected that the existence of both capacities in the
same individual should be rarer still. People who write
devotional verse are usually writing as they want to feel,
rather than as they do feel.'[1]

Eliot himself can never be accused of this lack of
integrity. He is acutely aware of the poet's creative burden
and the difficulty of communicating through language:

> Words strain,
> Crack and sometimes break, under the burden,
> Under the tension, slip, slide, perish,
> Decay with imprecision, will not stay in place,
> Will not stay still. Shrieking voices
> Scolding, mocking, or merely chattering,
> Always assail them. The Word in the desert
> Is most attacked by voices of temptation. . . .
> (*Burnt Norton*, V)

He admits almost to a sense of failure:

> So here I am, in the middle way, having had twenty years—
> Twenty years largely wasted, the years of *l'entre deux guerres*
> Trying to learn to use words, and every attempt
> Is a wholly new start, and a different kind of failure
> Because one has only learnt to get the better of words

[1] *After Strange Gods*, T. S. Eliot (Faber), p. 29

For the thing one no longer has to say, or the way in which
One is no longer disposed to say it. And so each venture
Is a new beginning, a raid on the inarticulate
With shabby equipment always deteriorating
In the general mess of imprecision of feeling,
Undisciplined squads of emotion.

(East Coker, V)

For the remainder of this chapter we shall limit our
attention to the work of two or three modern poets and
examine poems which use overt Christian symbols and
those using non-Christian symbols in a religious way.
This inevitably means that vast areas of poetic literature
will be unexplored but it is necessary, for reasons of space,
to concentrate on a few extended examples from poets
such as Eliot and Muir, in the hope that through this
more intensive study of a selected range we may begin to
see ways in which the whole subject may be treated. The
omission, however, of any detailed reference to poets from
the past like Dante, Milton, Herbert, and Donne, or to
Yeats or Hopkins from the present century, need not
preclude their work being read, studied, and compared
with the examples which have been selected.

The frequent references to T. S. Eliot in this book are
some indication of his position as Christian poet, critic and
dramatist, and many would claim that he is the outstanding Christian poet of the century. To read his poems in
the order in which they were written is to trace his spiritual
autobiography from agnosticism to the Christian faith.
His first work was published in 1917, when other poets
were either writing of the horrors of war, or of an escape
from it. Eliot's poems made no reference to the war, but

did speak of futility, of the sense of emptiness and frustration affecting all classes of society:

> Let us take the air, in a tobacco trance,
> Admire the monuments,
> Discuss the late events,
> Correct our watches by the public clocks.
> Then sit for half an hour and drink our bocks.
>
> *(Portrait of a Lady)*

> They are rattling breakfast plates in basement kitchens,
> And along the trampled edges of the street
> I am aware of the damp souls of housemaids
> Sprouting despondently at area gates.
>
> *(Morning at the Window)*

There is also futility in the Church—a church like that of the Laodiceans with a tepid faith, neither cold nor hot, existing on phrases and traditions which have lost their meaning and power:

> The hippo's feeble steps may err
> In compassing material ends,
> While the True Church need never stir
> To gather in its dividends. . . .

> The hippopotamus's day
> Is passed in sleep; at night he hunts;
> God works in a mysterious way—
> The Church can sleep and feed at once. . . .

At the end of the poem, it is the hippopotamus who rises to glory:

> He shall be washed as white as snow,
> By all the martyr'd virgins kist,
> While the True Church remains below
> Wrapt in the old miasmal mist.
>
> *(The Hippopotamus)*

H

These thoughts of disillusion and futility, of the rootlessness of modern man find their most complete expression in the extended poem *The Waste Land*, published in 1922 and received with some alarm by a public accustomed to the poetry of Rupert Brooke or John Masefield, and to the cricket and ale world of the Georgians. Two constant characteristics of Eliot's poetry are evident in this work. The first is his use of images and symbols in a way that went beyond that of the Imagists, who used images only in a precise visual sense. In Eliot, the image speaks not only of the quality of what it denotes (as 'dry stone' and 'stony rubbish' convey notions of aridity and barrenness), but it also has overtones which come from its references, sometimes obscure, at other times more immediately obvious, to earlier passages in other literature or mythology.

> What are the roots that clutch, what branches grow
> Out of this stony rubbish? Son of man,
> You cannot say, or guess, for you know only
> A heap of broken images, where the sun beats,
> And the dead tree gives no shelter, the cricket no relief,
> And the dry stone no sound of water.

(l. 19–24)

Eliot appended seven pages of notes to the poem, and some critics have argued that this in itself points to a danger in using images which cannot readily be understood. On the lines quoted above he refers his readers to passages in Ecclesiastes Ch. 12, and Ezekiel Ch. 2; and he could have added Ezekiel Ch. 37, where the prophet sees a valley of dry bones. The images are, indeed, 'broken.' Even the Christian story is stale news:

After the torchlight red on sweaty faces
After the frosty silence in the gardens
After the agony in stony places
The shouting and the crying
Prison and palace and reverberation
Of thunder of spring over distant mountains
He who was living is now dead
We who were living are now dying
With a little patience.

((l. 322–330)

All is not without hope. For after Gethsemane, there is Emmaus:

Who is the third who walks always beside you?
When I count, there are only you and I together
But when I look ahead up the white road
There is always another one walking beside you
Gliding wrapt in a brown mantle, hooded
I do not know whether a man or a woman
—But who is that on the other side of you?

(l. 359–365)

This is one characteristic of Eliot's style, the images that speak on two, or even more, levels. The other feature is his constant reference to the contrast, the paradox between two kinds of life and two kinds of death. A meaningless life is a living death; sacrificial death can be an awakening to life. It is an echo of 'He that saves his life shall lose it; and he that loses his life, for my sake, shall find it.'

This paradox is felt more fully in his later works, especially in the *Four Quartets*, which after *Ash Wednesday* (his first explicitly Christian poem) and the plays, represent an extended meditation on time and eternity, on the intersection of the timeless with time.

> At the still point of the turning world. Neither flesh nor
>   fleshless;
> Neither from nor towards; at the still point, there the dance is,
> But neither arrest nor movement. And do not call it fixity,
> Where past and future are gathered. Neither movement
>   from nor towards,
> Neither ascent nor decline. Except for the point, the still
>   point,
> There would be no dance, and there is only the dance.
>   *(Burnt Norton, II)*

As the fourth quartet moves to its close, there is a mood of
great calm and peace:

> We shall not cease from exploration
> And the end of all our exploring
> Will be to arrive where we started
> And know the place for the first time. . . .
> A condition of complete simplicity
> (Costing not less than everything)
> And all shall be well and
> All manner of thing shall be well
> When the tongues of flame are in-folded
> Into the crowned knot of fire
> And the fire and the rose are one.
>   *(Little Gidding, V)*

One of the most popular and easily understood of Eliot's
poems is *Journey of the Magi*, a sharp and vivid reconstruction of the hardships facing the travellers to Bethlehem:

> A cold coming we had of it,
> Just the worst time of the year
> For a journey, and such a long journey . . .
> . . . the camel men cursing and grumbling
> And running away, and wanting their liquor and women,
> And the night-fires going out, and the lack of shelters,
> And the cities hostile and the towns unfriendly
> And the villages dirty and charging high prices:

A hard time we had of it.
At the end we preferred to travel all night,
Sleeping in snatches,
With the voices singing in our ears, saying
That this was all folly.

And at the end of the poem, spoken, as it were, many
years later, one of the wise men wonders about the
meaning of what they saw:

All this was a long time ago, I remember,
And I would do it again, but set down
This set down
This: were we led all that way for
Birth or Death? There was a Birth, certainly,
We had evidence and no doubt. I had seen birth and death,
But had thought they were different; this Birth was
Hard and bitter agony for us, like Death, our death.
We returned to our places, these Kingdoms,
But no longer at ease here, in the old dispensation,
With an alien people clutching their gods.
I should be glad of another death.

The paradox is still present, but it is more obviously
stated, and Eliot's use of capitals makes clear the significance of the Birth which causes the death of the old self
and the dissatisfaction with the old, dying order.

Eliot has so dominated English poetry for more than a
generation that it is easy to ignore other work. But it is
interesting to compare, say, *Journey of the Magi* and *A Song
for Simeon*, both associated with the festival of Christmas,
with another treatment of that festival by Louis MacNeice,
in *Autumn Journal*:

A week to Christmas, cards of snow and holly,
    Gimcracks in the shops,
Wishes and memories wrapped in tissue paper,
    Trinkets, gadgets and lollipops

And as if through coloured glasses
   We remember our childhood's thrill
Waking in the morning to the rustling of paper,
   The eiderdown heaped in a hill
Of wogs and dogs and bears and bricks and apples
   And the feeling that Christmas Day
Was a coral island in time where we land and eat our lotus
   But where we can never stay.
There was a star in the East, the magi in their turbans
   Brought their luxury toys
In homage to a child born to capsize their values
   And wreck their equipoise.
A smell of hay like peace in a dark stable—
   Not peace however but a sword
To cut the Gordian knot of logical self-interest,
   The fool-proof golden cord;
For Christ walked in where no philosopher treads
   But armed with more than folly,
Making the smooth place rough and knocking the heads
   Of Church and State together.
In honour of whom we have taken over the pagan
   Saturnalia for our annual treat
Letting the belly have its say, ignoring
   The spirit while we eat.
And Conscience still goes crying through the desert
   With sackcloth round his loins:
A week to Christmas—hark the herald angels
   Beg for copper coins.

When Eliot exposed a world arid with unbelief he
looked beyond the disillusion to hope. A poet of the
present generation, Philip Larkin, expresses well a disillusion which is an end in itself:

      Strange to know nothing, never to be sure
      Of what is true or right or real,
      But forced to qualify *or so I feel*,
      Or *Well, it does seem so:*
      Someone must know. . . .

Yes, it is strange,
Even to wear such knowledge—for our flesh
Surrounds us with its own decisions—
And yet spend all our life on imprecisions,
That when we start to die
Have no idea why.

(*Ignorance*)

And where Eliot used the hippopotamus to poke fun at
the Church, in *Church Going*, Larkin sees churches as the
dying relics of an almost defunct superstition. The poet
visits a small country church, looks round, then—

                              Back at the door
I sign the book, donate an Irish sixpence,
Reflect the place was not worth stopping for.

Yet stop I did: in fact I often do,
And always end much at a loss like this,
Wondering what to look for; wondering, too,
When churches fall completely out of use
What we shall turn them into, if we shall keep
A few cathedrals chronically on show,
Their parchment, plate and pyx in locked cases,
And let the rest rent-free to rain and sheep.
Shall we avoid them as unlucky places?

Or, after dark, will dubious women come
To make their children touch a particular stone;
Pick simples for a cancer; or on some
Advised night see walking a dead one?
Power of some sort or other will go on
In games, in riddles, seemingly at random;
But superstition, like belief, must die,
And what remains when disbelief has gone?
Grass, weedy pavement, brambles, buttress, sky,

A shape less recognisable each week,
A purpose more obscure.

The other poet whose work we shall look at in some detail is Edwin Muir, who died in 1959. Muir, like Eliot, was a convert. Like Eliot also, though in a different manner, he used myth to provide clues and pointers to the Christian Faith. Many of the poems in *The Labyrinth* and *One Foot in Eden* refer to Greek and Hebrew mythology, and in his work he is concerned with the basic themes: God and Man, the Fall, birth and death, time and eternity. 'As I look back upon the part of the mystery which is my own life, my own fable, what I am most aware of is that we receive more than we can ever give; we receive it from the past, on which we draw with every breath, but also—and this is the point of faith, from the source of the mystery itself, by the means which religious people call Grace.'[1]

Three of Muir's later poems refer to events in the Gospels and attempt to comment on the inner meaning and truth of them: *The Annunciation*, *The Transfiguration*, and *The Killing*. The first is a short poem of intense ecstasy; in the second he speaks, in describing the effect of the Transfiguration on the disciples, of the penetrating vision that perceives the divine glory:

> So from the ground we felt that virtue branch
> Through all our veins till we were whole, our wrists
> As fresh and pure as water from a well,
> Our hands made new to handle holy things,
> The source of all our seeing rinsed and cleansed
> Till earth and light and water entering there
> Gave back to us the clear unfallen world.

[1] *Autobiography*, Edwin Muir (Hogarth Press), p. 281

This vision of glory is something which poets of every age have seen and proclaimed: There is Dante's vision of light shining through light:

> As lightning startles vision from the eyes,
>   Leaving them empty of capacity
>   The clearest images to visualise
> So now a living light encompassed me;
>   In veil so luminous I was enwrapt
>   That naught, swathed in such glory, could I see.
>
> (*Paradiso* xxx, 46-51)

And Wordsworth, in *Intimations of Immortality*:

> There was a time when meadow, grove, and stream
>   The earth, and every common sight,
>   To me did seem
>   Apparelled in celestial light,
> The glory and the freshness of a dream.

Muir comments about his own poem: 'I had always been deeply struck by the story of the Transfiguration in the Gospels, and I had felt that perhaps at the moment of Christ's transfiguration everything was transfigured, mankind, and the animals, and the simplest natural objects.' Muir describes this transfiguration with compelling power and beauty. But is it an illusion?

> Was it a vision?
> Or did we see that day the unseeable
> One glory of the everlasting world
> Perpetually at work, though never seen
> Since Eden locked the gate that's everywhere
> And nowhere? Was the change in us alone,
> And the enormous earth still left forlorn,
> An exile or a prisoner?

This transfiguration, this perception, is akin to the artistic experience—when the artist with paint, words, music or stone opens our eyes to things which surround us but which we never notice. So the reading of a poem, the hearing of some music, becomes a moment of disclosure:

> Reality or vision, this we have seen.
> If it had lasted but another moment
> It might have held for ever! But the world
> Rolled back into its place, and we are here,
> And all that radiant kingdom lies forlorn,
> As if it had never stirred.

It is not only the natural order that is transformed; man too is released and renewed:

> And when we went into the town, he with us,
> The lurkers under doorways, murderers,
> With rags tied round their feet for silence, came
> Out of themselves to us and were with us . . .
> And those entangled in their own devices,
> The silent and the garrulous liars, all
> Stepped out of their dungeons and were free.

The poem concludes with a glimpse of a day when this order of things will be the permanent order, when Christ returns:

> Then he will come, Christ the uncrucified,
> Christ the discrucified, his death undone,
> His agony unmade, his cross dismantled—
> Glad to be so—and the tormented wood
> Will cure its hurt and grow into a tree
> In a green springing corner of young Eden,
> And Judas damned take his long journey backward
> From darkness into light and be a child
> Beside his mother's knee, and the betrayal
> Be quite undone and never more be done.

The Killing is a moving portrayal of the last hours of Our Lord on Calvary. After the description of the scene there follows, as in *Journey of the Magi*, the question, probing for the inner meaning.

That was the day they killed the Son of God
On a squat hill-top by Jerusalem.
Zion was bare, her children from their maze
Sucked by the demon curiosity
Clean through the gates. The very halt and blind
Had somehow got themselves up to the hill. . . .

We watched the writhings, heard the moanings, saw
The three heads turning on their separate axles
Like broken wheels left spinning. Round *his* head
Was loosely bound a crown of plaited thorn
That hurt at random, stinging temple and brow
As the pain swung into its envious circle.
In front the wreath was gathered in a knot
That as he gazed looked like the last stump left
Of a death-wounded deer's great antlers. . . .

  The sun revolved, the shadow wheeled,
The evening fell. His head lay on his breast,
But in his breast they watched his heart move on
By itself alone, accomplishing its journey.
Their taunts grew louder, sharpened by the knowledge
That he was walking in the park of death,
Far from their rage. Yet all grew stale at last,
Spite, curiosity, envy, hate itself.
They waited only for death and death was slow
And came so quietly they scarce could mark it.
They were angry then with death and death's deceit.

I was a stranger, could not read these people
Or this outlandish deity. Did a God
Indeed in dying cross my life that day
By chance, he on his road and I on mine?

7. Drama

> 1st SHEPHERD: Let us make haste, then, e'en to the stable to see the babe!
>
> 2nd SHEPHERD: Aye, let us go and take unto him our gifts, for on this day we ought to make merry and be right joyful.
>
>   (*Exeunt* shepherds, carrying lambs)

THOSE WORDS are not taken from a particular play, but they might easily occur in any of the hundreds of static, tableaux-like nativity plays which are staged each year and which to some people are synonymous with Christian drama. Many of these plays may have as little claim to be regarded as Christian drama, as the saccharine type Madonna of the Christmas card has to be regarded as Christian art, or the sentimental seasonal ballad as Christian music. We have already seen that merely to use Christian symbols and language does not, of necessity, produce a religious or Christian work of art, and it may well be that in our contemporary theatre as in the novel, the most truly religious works may have little apparent connection with specifically Christian terminology.

In the middle ages the words 'Christian' or 'religious' were unnecessary adjectives—The Drama implied the re-enactment of the Gospel story, a setting forth of the 'mystery' of man's salvation, and in terms of the medieval plays this ranged from Creation to the Last Judgment. Indeed, our national drama came out of the worship of the Church, with its roots in the simplest dramatic dialogue and action of the Easter liturgy. Beyond the Christian drama there were the ancient mystery religions from which the Greek drama sprang, with its ritual song and dance. Quite apart from religious and Christian origins of drama, there is an essential unity between religion and drama—they are both concerned with 'incarnation,' making the word flesh, the invisible visible, and representing the interpenetration of two worlds—two worlds no longer separate because of the action of God in Christ.

As in so many other fields, the medieval unity was shattered by the fragmentation and secularization of the Renaissance and in England (inspired by such texts as Deut. 22. 5) the later aversion of the Puritan movement to the theatre as an instrument of the world, the flesh and the devil, led to a further estrangement of the two. This strict compartment-mentality, the separation of 'religion' into one box and 'life' or 'the theatre' into another, is only now beginning to be broken down, and any appraisal of modern religious drama must take account of at least three types of play: the specifically Christian play, often written for a sympathetic audience and performed in a church, such as *Murder in the Cathedral*; the play written by an avowed Christian but using a secular symbolism, such as *The Cocktail Party* or *The Dark is Light Enough*; and the play written by an author who may not be a Christian but who is showing us something of the condition of man and his need, such as *Waiting for Godot*, *A View from the Bridge*, or *A Taste of Honey*. Before looking at some of these works in more detail we shall consider what is the aim of the Christian dramatist.

Articles in the journal *Christian Drama* reveal a surprising conflict of views on this point. One playwright maintains that there is no essential difference between religious drama and other sorts of drama, whilst another argues that the Christian dramatist's aim is conversion and that 'the spectator of a Christian drama should go away in the sure and certain hope of the consequences to himself of the historical Resurrection.' A theologian warns of the distinction between drama as an art form and the teaching and preaching office of the church—the two should not be confused and we should not have plays that preach at us. An English critic argues that a 'Christian play resembles a socialist or other politically governed play—it is committed to propaganda. It is a weapon of conversion . . . and in a sense something hostile to a work of art. This may be the reason why there are so few good ones.'

Now it is inevitable that a Christian writer be partisan in so far as his faith affects his interpretation of life and his way of looking at things and people. Yet as an artist he has a concern for the integrity and the autonomy of his art and he must resist the tendency to use his play as a vehicle for 'getting ideas across,' for assuming the role of preacher and teacher. It is this didactic streak which is one of the weaknesses of *The Living Room* when, at the end of the play, Greene uses the aged priest to 'moralize' and comment on the tragedy of Rose's suicide. It is as if he is afraid to let the audience draw its own conclusions in case they are the wrong ones. Well, that is a risk that any work of art must take. Jesus notably refrained from pointing the moral of his parables. They, like their author, had their own authority which could be accepted or rejected.

In one respect the religious dramatist is helped in that the basic structure and rhythm of classical tragedy provides

a mould already shaped to the themes of death and
resurrection. A play begins with the hero-figure portrayed
as one kind of man; he suffers because he is this kind of
person, and perhaps because of the sins of others as well
as his own; and through his suffering he emerges as a
different kind of person. In a sense, he dies and is reborn.
This happens in Eliot's *Family Reunion* (modelled closely
on the Greek tragedy, *The Oresteia*), or Ibsen's *Brand*, or
Marcel's *A Man of God*. And plays are not merely meant
to be read. They are performed to audiences who share
in the cathartic experience of tragedy which Aristotle
described: that the soul should be purged by pity and
terror—the terror, for the Christian, of the pain of passing
through death to life. If this is true, it is immaterial
whether the period is biblical or contemporary; the
language Elizabethan or modern. The play's 'religious'
quality does not depend on these factors at all. Indeed,
the biblical setting often merely deceives and confuses the
audience. For the truly religious (as distinct from the
religiose) play puts the contemporary world in touch
with the eternal world; an incarnation takes place and we,
in the audience, share in it. It is 'religious' because it
concerns 'involvement,' God's involvement in the sin and
suffering of humanity, and the involvement of the children
of God, whether we acknowledge it or not.

We can therefore conveniently divide modern drama
into three sections. There are, first of all, those plays
which are quite openly concerned with Christian themes
and values and use a religious setting for their action. In
this country the most notable of these is *Murder in the
Cathedral*, written expressly for performance in Canterbury

Cathedral in 1935. It had an immediate appeal, the atmosphere of doom and the realization of sin stated in the fine verse writing for the chorus voicing the mood of many people at the time.

> Here let us stand, close by the Cathedral. Here let us wait.
> Are we drawn by danger? Is it the knowledge of safety that draws
> Our feet towards the Cathedral? What danger can be
> For us, the poor, the poor women of Canterbury?

In the face of the menace to their Archbishop they are aware of their inadequacy, their compromise, their desire only for peace:

> We do not wish anything to happen.
> Seven years we have lived quietly,
> Succeeded in avoiding notice,
> Living and partly living.

The Zeal of Thy House, by D. L. Sayers, was written in 1937, also for performance at Canterbury, and post-war plays by Christopher Fry, Norman Nicholson and R. H. Ward have continued to explore this field of religious drama.

It is true that these plays often make a great impact on the congregation, but there is an inevitable limitation in both theme and structure when plays are written mainly for performance in a church setting. And there is a danger, too, that the division between the religious and the secular is emphasised, with sincere Christian playwrights writing plays suitable for churches and acceptable to the devout, while others, in the open world of the secular theatre, grapple with the problems of man's identity and relevance.

This criticism does not apply to Eliot, however, whose later plays were designed for the secular theatre using the conventions of the West End 'society' play of his period. And this brings us to the second type of religious drama, in which the Christian faith is set forth in apparently non-Christian terms. Eliot's second play was *Family Reunion*, in which he used a chorus, as in Greek drama, but set the action in a north country house with a family concerned with their guilt, and with Henry and Agatha realizing that one person's full acceptance of suffering may free another from doom, and release atoning power. The theological nuances and the ritual are only thinly disguised and we are still very much in the field of Christian thought. But with *The Cocktail Party*, *The Confidential Clerk*, and *The Elder Statesman*, Eliot uses the machinery of the drawing-room comedy as a device for portraying the Christian themes of salvation and damnation.

The setting of *The Cocktail Party* is the sophisticated social life of upper middle class people where sin is examined in terms of psychological disturbance and hell is experienced as a nervous breakdown. Lavinia and Edward are drifting apart in their marriage and are seeking some consolation in love affairs. As the play opens, Lavinia has left Edward and he comes to realize that though he is now in a position to make more permanent his relationship with Celia, his mistress, he does not really wish to do this. His dilemma lies between having a wife he does not love and a woman he is incapable of loving. There is a stranger at a cocktail party at Edward's house and he begins to reveal and offer solutions for this abuse and inadequacy of love. He is a psychiatrist and to his consulting room go the three main characters. Edward

and Lavinia come to see that a kind of love is possible
between them; there can be reconciliation, of a sort.
They

> Are contented with the morning that separates
> And with the evening that brings together
> For casual talk before the fire
> Two people who know they do not understand each other,
> Breeding children whom they do not understand
> And who will never understand them.

This may seem a rather negative life, though the
psychiatrist suggests that 'in a world of lunacy, violence,
stupidity, greed . . . it is a good life.'

But for Ceilia there is a more difficult choice to make.
She has realized that love has been abused.

> I found we were only strangers
> And that there had been neither giving nor taking
> But that we had merely made use of each other
> Each for his purpose. That's horrible. Can we only love
> Something created by our own imagination?

She feels there must be a purer love than this:

> In which one is exalted by intensity of loving
> In the spirit, a vibration of delight
> Without desire, for desire is fulfilled
> In the delight of loving.

She is given a choice: she can be 'reconciled to the
human condition'—the way Edward and Lavinia have
chosen—or she can take a leap of faith—'the kind of faith
that issues from despair.'

> The destination cannot be described;
> You will know very little until you get there;
> You will journey blind.
> But the way leads towards possession
> Of what you have sought for in the wrong place.

She decides for this unknown way and is sent to the 'sanatorium' from which she later goes abroad as a missionary, and suffers a frightful death by martyrdom. It is the news of this death which comes to the other characters, assembled for another cocktail party, at the close of the play and Edward and Lavinia feel that they 'are somehow involved in the wrong.' But the psychiatrist describes Celia's course as one of suffering which led to victory—a *via crucis*:

> Because you think her death was wasted
> You blame yourselves, and because you blame yourselves
> You think her life was wasted. It was triumphant.
> But I am no more responsible for the triumph—
> And just as responsible for her death as you are.

Despite the cocktail party atmosphere there are moments of deliberate religious symbolism, most notably a libation that is drunk to Celia by the psychiatrist and his two assistants, who have the air of guardian angels:

> Watch over her in the desert.
> Watch over her in the mountain.
> Watch over her in the labyrinth.
> Watch over her by the quicksand.

And his final words to her are:

> Go in peace, my daughter.
> Work out your own salvation with diligence.

Although the play can be faulted both in its theology (in that it suggests a double standard of morality, the higher and the lower way) and in its dramatic structure, yet it remains a bold attempt to present the theme of salvation in a situation and language which is immediate and contemporary; and in a society dominated by matrimonial misfits and affairs, it demonstrates the purification of the heart through love.

The 'compromise' solution of Edward and Lavinia and the 'living and partly living' of the women of Canterbury are very like the philosophy of the Sicilian lawyer in Arthur Miller's play, *A View from the Bridge*. The world of the Brooklyn waterfront is a far cry from Mayfair society, but there also they 'settle for half.' The truth of complete exposure and self-knowledge is too painful. Miller is always a compelling dramatist with a profound concern for the human condition, and the climax of this play comes with the fight between Eddie Carbone and Marco, the Sicilian immigrant whose brother is in love with Eddie's niece, Catherine, whom Eddie and his wife are caring for. The tragic flaw in Eddie's character is his hidden incestuous love for this niece and his reluctance to allow the marriage to proceed. This is the miserable truth which Eddie cannot face, and rather than admit it he courts personal disaster in the final conflict with Marco. In the fight Eddie is killed and as his wife and niece take up his body, Alfieri, the lawyer, acting as a chorus, comments on the struggling humanity he sees about him:

> Most of the time now we settle for half and I like it better. But the truth is holy, and even as I know how wrong he was, and his death useless, I tremble, for I confess that something perversely pure calls to me from his memory— not purely good, but himself purely, for he allowed himself to be wholly known and for that I think I will love him more than all my sensible clients. And yet, it is better to settle for half, it must be! And so I mourn him—I admit it —with a certain . . . alarm.

There are two other types of modern play that must be mentioned, for they deal with two problems of concern to the Christian—anger and communication.

'Angry young men' and 'kitchen-sink drama' have become not only the battle cries of the organizations that protest against 'filth on British TV screens,' but also the image of British drama since Jimmy Porter, the original Angry Young Man, walked the boards of the Royal Court Theatre on 8th May, 1956. Three years earlier, in *The Living Room*, Graham Greene, with typical attachment to the seedy, had the action and dialogue punctuated from time to time by the flushing of the toilet, backstage. But after *Look Back in Anger* the regular and almost essential setting of the New Wave plays appeared to be the sordid kitchen, attic, basement, even public lavatory, and the action ranged through promiscuity, homosexuality, and illegitimacy. The mood was often angry, with bitter searing attacks on the Establishment; protests against *Them*. How can we possibly consider such plays to be of importance in a discussion of Christian drama?

First, we cannot simply denounce anger. It is true that blind, unreasoning, unloving wrath is a hideous thing, and in some of the plays of this type this appears to be the dominant emotion. But not all anger is like this, and not all the playwrights are victims of a purely negative anger. At one point in *King Lear*, Kent proclaims that 'Anger hath a privilege.' In his case it is the privilege of denouncing the destruction of family love through the ruthlessness of Goneril and Regan's actions, and the shoddiness of Oswald their time-server. It is a noble rage against falseness and evil. And when it speaks it uses strong language.

Shakespeare has no monopoly of this fierce anger. It can be found in some of the most scathing attacks of the Old Testament Prophets on the hollowness and hypocrisy of their society:

> Hear this word, you cows of Bashan,
> Who are in the mountain of Samaria,
> Who oppress the poor, who crush the needy,
> Who say to their husbands, bring that we may drink.
> The days are coming upon you
> When they shall take you away with hooks,
> Even the last of you with fish hooks. . . .
>
> (Amos 4. 1–2)

And John the Baptist was not exactly smooth or polite when he greeted his audience at Jordan:

> You generation of vipers—who warned you to flee from the wrath to come? (Lk. 3. 7)

Jesus, too, was outspoken when the situation demanded it. He attacked the Pharisees for devouring the property of helpless widows, for covering themselves with white-wash on the outside to look good, when inside they were rotten, foul and stinking. (Mt. 23. 27)

Indeed, one of the causes of the anger of writers like Osborne is that society has become afraid of being passionately concerned, one way or another, about things. We are too content to 'settle for half' and we escape from the real business of living into our trivial conversations about the weather, or hide behind the pomposity of public attitudes. We have become, in Eliot's phrase, a generation of 'hollow men'—and it is a hollow civilization that the angry writers denounce. But this mission of denunciation can easily become an empty and frustrating activity, only negative and destructive. And we could say, I think, that there are three essential elements in a Christian anger of criticism: A Divine vocation in that my anger is justified because what I condemn is wrong in itself; a basic love for human beings, and a refusal to glory in the loneliness of the rebel for its own sake; and a humility which shows a readiness to admit that I may be wrong. Righteous Anger must always be balanced by its complementary quality of Divine Hope.

For all this, it would be a mistake to dismiss the 'angry plays' of the last decade as of no relevance to the Christian. In *Look Back in Anger*, for all the ranting against Bishops, the 'posh' Sunday papers and the Establishment, with Jimmy Porter wearing an outsized chip-on-the-shoulder, 'there is a plea for human honesty and vitality, for people to live emotionally as fully and as deeply as they can'. Towards the end of the play, Jimmy, in his frustration, voices his principal indictment of society:

> They all want to escape from the pain of being alive. And, most of all, from love. I always knew something like this would turn up—some problem, like an ill wife—and it would be too much for those delicate, hot-house feelings of yours. It's no good trying to fool yourself about love. You can't fall into it like a soft job, without dirtying up your hands. It takes muscle and guts. And if you can't bear the thought of messing up your nice, clean soul, you'd better give up the whole idea of life, and become a saint. Because you'll never make it as a human being. It's either this world or the next.

It is important to realize that although many of this group of writers are showing us in vivid terms the life of a certain section of society, they do not use their plays, with the possible exception of Wesker, as conscious vehicles for advocating social justice and reform. They rather see within this setting, which is a valid one for our age, both personal and universal themes working themselves out. *A Taste of Honey*, for instance, might easily be dismissed at a superficial level. The setting is a sleazy Salford flat, within spitting distance of the gasworks and the docks. Jo, an adolescent girl, lives with her mother who, after several affairs with different men, is about to marry one of them, a drunken lout, while she can. Her mother away for the honeymoon, Jo is left alone and falls in love with a coloured sailor who is on leave. She becomes pregnant, and is helped through her pregnancy by a young homosexual art student. When mother returns she gets rid of the student and is horrified to discover Jo's child may be black.

Stated baldly without the dialogue and atmosphere of the play, this seems to be an indulgence in the sordid for its own sake. Yet beneath and through this experience (and the colour problem, illegitimacy and marital unfaithfulness are only too common features of our society), we realize that the play is concerned about love, and Jo's awareness of different kinds of love—the feeling she has for the coloured boy, the compassionate concern which the student can offer her when she is in need, and the love which she discovers she bears for her child.

If some modern plays seem unpleasant, others appear to be futile and meaningless. After having listened for an evening to what seems to be completely inconsequential dialogue, mainly monosyllabic, with very little action at all, some theatregoers begin to wonder if, as in the case of some modern art, they are being taken for a ride. What they have failed to see is that in dispensing with the

embellishments of rhetoric and décor the author is inviting
them to attend 'a naked enquiry into the being of Man
and the nature of God.'

Waiting for Godot is a play about two tramps. They are
on the stage for the whole play, and beside them on a
mound is a tree. They are waiting, so they inform us, for
a Mr. Godot who has promised to come to them and
whose arrival they believe will solve all their worries and
problems. They discuss life, a futile affair without meaning. At last two travellers appear, Pozzo and his servant
Lucky, tied by a cord round his neck and carrying Pozzo's
luggage. At one point Lucky is told to think and he
begins a long speech of confused incoherence, images and
words tumbling out one after the other. They leave, and
Vladimir and Estragon, the two tramps, remain, still
waiting for Godot, who, so a messenger comes to tell
them, will not be coming this evening, but will arrive
tomorrow.

The second act is similar in structure to the first. The
two tramps still wait—Pozzo and Lucky reappear but
now Pozzo is blind. Lucky sleeps by the tree, and later
rises and leads Pozzo away. The tramps continue to
wait, and a second messenger comes to say that Mr. Godot
won't be coming, and the curtain falls as they wait for
an event which we all feel will never happen.

To some, especially in view of Beckett's later plays,
with legless characters in dustbins, this was an attempt to
see how gullible an audience can be. But this does not
explain the power and impact the play made and continues to make on audiences. And there are strange hints
of religious symbols throughout the play. There is a
conversation between the tramps about the two thieves at

Calvary and when Estragon takes off his boots, which are too small, and leaves them, Vladimir says to him:

V.: But you can't go barefoot!
E.: Christ did.
V.: Christ! What's Christ got to do with it? You're not going to compare yourself to Christ!
E.: All my life I've compared myself to him.
V.: But where he was it was warm, it was dry!
E.: Yes. And they crucified quick.

And if we try to reduce Lucky's 'nonsense' speech to a sentence, he is saying:

> Given the existence of a personal God who loves us and suffers and considering that, as a result of labours left unfinished, Man wastes and pines—I resume, in a Word, the Skull.

Does this mean that the play approaches a Christian statement? The author is no orthodox Christian, and this is certainly not 'religious drama' in any formal sense. But K. M. Baxter, in *Speak what we feel*, has made out a strong case for seeing in this play a distinct resemblance to the structure of a Passion play Mr. Godot may or may not resemble God—the *deus ex machina* whom the tramps await as a solution to all their problems. Yet while they wait, God does come, in the person of Lucky, the despised 'suffering servant,' with no form or comeliness (a hideous sore festers on his neck where the rope cuts into the flesh). He bears the rubbishy gear of Pozzo (later identified by the tramps as mankind). Lucky appears to die at the tree, the place of the skull. 'To hell with him,' says Estragon. And in the second act the tree begins to bear leaves, the tree is a tree of life; Pozzo, blind mankind, is led by Lucky, refreshed and raised from his sleep, into the city. For the tramps the significance is not clear, as Vladimir reveals in his final speech:

> Was I sleeping, while the others suffered? Am I sleeping now? Tomorrow when I wake, or think I do, what shall I say of today? That with Estragon, my friend, at this place, until the fall of night, I waited for Godot? That Pozzo passed, with his carrier, and talked to us? Probably. But in all that what truth will there be? . . . Astride of a grave and a difficult birth. Down in the hole, lingeringly, the grave-digger puts on the forceps. We have time to grow old. . . .

It may be felt that this interpretation reads far too much into the play and that this is not what Beckett consciously intended. That it is as absurd as to suggest that *Three Blind Mice* is an allegory for the Trinity. On the other hand, is it not possible to see in this tale of suffering a reflection of the archetype of suffering; to see in this experience, however unconscious and disguised, a reflection of the *motif* of suffering which springs from the Christian faith. Other plays, it is true, do not offer such sympathetic examples. Indeed, much of the drama of writers like Ionesco and Pinter seems to portray only a negative way of frustration. Ionesco's *Rhinoceros* is a protest against the 'Organization Man' pressures in modern society. We all conform, until in the end if we insist on retaining our individuality, in remaining human, we shall become monsters. All the characters in the play have turned into rhinoceroses except Bérenger:

> *They're* the good looking ones. . . . How I wish I was like them . . . now its too late, now I'm a monster . . . just a monster . . . People who try to hang on to their individuality always come to a bad end. Oh, well, too bad. I'll take on

all of them. I'll put up a fight against the lot of them, the whole lot of them. I'm the last man left, and I'm staying that way until the end, I'm not capitulating.

The author makes his point with the absurd and the grotesque—humans changing into rhinos, and in *Amédée*, a corpse, left for years in a room in the flat of a middle aged couple, starts to grow and push its feet and legs into the living room. It is a symbol of the guilt and lovelessness that haunts their life, and from which they cannot escape. For Ionesco, not only language, but things, communicate and speak. Indeed, silence frightens people and language is an escape from reality. He is quoted as saying that as man 'is not alone in the world, and as each of us is, deep down, everyone else, one man's dreams, longings, anxieties and obsessions do not belong to him alone. They are part of an ancestral heritage. It is this that constitutes our profound one-ness and our universal language.' So we are driven down beneath the superficial ripples that disguise the true condition of man.

There is a negative quality about these plays that leaves the Christian dissatisfied and ill at ease. It is as if they bring us to a point of diagnosis, of painful analysis, and then leave us there. They show man as alone, afraid, submerged in the herd, overcome by guilt—so that we are driven to voice the despair of St. Paul who seeing the horror of man in his sin cried out: 'Who shall deliver me from this body of death?' There is no slick or easy answer, though that is not to say there is *no* answer. Paul's answer was given in the eighth chapter of his letter to the Romans, an exposition of the love of God, actively involved in the human predicament, suffering as only

love can suffer when it faces evil; suffering, but not overcome, not defeated. It is this dimension that is lacking in
much of our modern drama and this is not surprising in
a society which has ceased to accept the Christian faith
as its guiding philosophy.

But there are some plays which speak not only of man's
plight but point a way to his deliverance—such works as
The Dark is Light Enough, by Christopher Fry, or *The
Carmelites*, by Henri Bernanos. In the former, the villain,
Gettner, is saved through the Countess's persistent faith
and love; in the latter, set within the Order of the Carmelites, a nun, Blanche, obsessed with fear, is able to face
death unafraid because of the offering of her former
Prioress's life. In each case, we witness Easter, which the
theologian Rudolf Bultmann well describes as the 'rising
of faith.' 'The life of faith,' says Bultmann, 'is to open
ourselves freely to the future. In bringing a man to faith
the love of God treats man as other than he is, embraces
and sustains him even in his fallen self-assertive state, and
so frees him from himself as he is, to be what he was
intended to be.' This is precisely the service which the
women who in these plays are the agents of the love of
God perform for Gettner and Blanche de la Force.

'They are redeemed by the self-offering of others—they
bear within themselves the principle of their own destruction, and have to be transfigured through the sacrificial
act of another. So in each play we see the sinner, the
person who is in danger of missing the mark, brought out
of despair, absolved, loosed from bondage, reinstated.'[1]

It is a far cry from the ecclesiastical setting of *Murder in
the Cathedral* in 1935 to the stage of the Royal Court

[1] *Speak what we feel*, K. M. Baxter (S.C.M.), p. 76-77

Theatre in 1957, with two dustbins holding the remnants of Nell and Nagg in Beckett's *Endgame*. Yet we have seen that between these two apparent extremes the serious drama of the last twenty years has been concerned with the basic themes of religious thought.

'It is by no means orthodox; indeed it calls in question many of the surface assumptions of the ordinary church-goer. Yet, if we believe that the Christian doctrine of the Incarnation gives the pattern of New Life, the doctrine of the Trinity the pattern of relationship of persons, the Atonement the pattern of forgiveness and openness to the future, and Calvary the pattern of the stripping required before man can make the leap into Resurrection —if we believe this, we must agree that dramatists today are grappling with man's deep need for God.'[1]

[1] *London Quarterly Review*, K. M. Baxter, Oct. 1960, p. 286

8. Cinema

No BOOK on the arts in the twentieth century would be complete without a section on the cinema. The film is the only major art form to have arisen within the century and it is not surprising that in an age in which the arts generally have not sought inspiration from Biblical subjects this newest form has not yet learned to transpose the Bible into its own medium. This is not to say that there are no religious films, as we shall see later; but rather that ironically the Biblical films are not the religious ones. Indeed, they damage the cause of real religion and often offend informed Christian people.

The cinema as an art form is highly complex. It has obvious affinities with the theatre and draws much of its material from fiction, but it is a medium which has developed its distinctive disciplines and is an art form in its own right, so that it is no longer possible to think of a film as merely a cinematic version of a play or novel. Indeed, Tennessee Williams, many of whose plays have been made into films, admired the cinema for being 'better for exploring the mid-century obsessions. They have suddenly discovered how to use the camera to suggest things the stage can't. It's more penetrating, the poetry of suggestion. . . . These subtle changes they can give in close-ups of faces. The theatre must learn from the cinema, try to get back to lost sensibilities. Dramatists must use these new techniques.'[1]

[1] *The Observer*, 28 March, 1965

One difficulty in discussing films is that the only films some people may have seen are the box-office successes of Hollywood, the traditional British comedies or the dreary stale films of Sunday television programmes. It is rather like trying to discuss the art of the novel if one has only read Micky Spillane, Ian Fleming and an occasional cheap and abridged version of the classics. This does not mean that a box-office success need not be a commanding film, though the pressures of commercial interests tend to effect a compromise in the making of such films. But the great majority of films that are on the cinema circuits of the country will not, for instance, be examples of what a French critic once called the *Camera Stylo*, the camera as a fountain-pen. 'This image has a very precise sense. It means that the cinema will break away little by little from the tyranny of the visual, of the image for its own sake, of the immediate anecdote, of the concrete, to become a means of writing as supple and as subtle as that of written language. No area must be barred to it. The most austere meditation, attitudes to all human works, psychology, metaphysics, ideas, passions are very precisely its province. Indeed, these ideas and visions of the world are such that today the cinema alone is capable of giving them full realization.'[1]

There are other difficulties which arise in film appreciation and criticism. If a critic refers to passages from a novel or poem, or to a great painting or piece of music, it is not difficult to look up the passage or picture and study it in detail. But if we have not seen the film that is being discussed it is difficult to appreciate the validity of any statements made about it. Even when we have seen

[1] *Cinema Eye, Cinema Ear*, J. R. Taylor (Methuen), p. 14

the film, we have probably seen it only once. It is true that the initial impact of a film, a play or a piece of music might be a moving experience. But we would not normally feel in a position to pass an informed judgment on, say, a Beethoven symphony if we had heard it only once. Indeed, the greater the work of art, the more it repays a detailed and prolonged acquaintance. Despite these difficulties, however, we shall have to consider a number of films, some of them foreign, in this discussion. Many of them can be hired for private showing on 16 mm. machines; literature on the cinema including journals such as *Sight and Sound* and the *British Film Bulletin* often gives synopses as well as criticisms of the works; while the British Film Institute will promote discussion programmes using excerpts from films which cover some of the topics mentioned below. Even if these facilities are not available we can still look at films with an intelligent and informed interest; with, for example, the same critical awareness that we might give to a novel by Graham Greene or a play by Beckett, paying attention not only to the central situation which the film portrays but to the techniques which the director is using to establish this situation in a convincing manner.

There is another difference between the cinema and the other arts. We discuss novels in terms of their writers, buildings in terms of their architects, pictures in terms of their painters. But who is the artist behind the film? So far as the advertising agency is concerned it often seems to be the leading actor; the star billing will draw in the crowds. But as we well know from the first two minutes of every film, the credit titles seem to be endless and indicate the number of people—script writers, composers,

K

cameramen, editors, as well as the actors—who have been included in the making of the film. Some films may well be actors' films and we can talk in terms of seeing 'O'Toole's *Lawrence of Arabia*'; but there will occasionally be films when other characteristics become dominant— the script, the music, the camera work, the sets and location. And if the public relations men in Wardour Street talk in terms of the 'stars', the critics' columns tend to mention the directors (or in the U.S.A., the producers) —Fellini, Bergman, Hitchcock, or Losey. It is usually these men who have the vision of what they wish to create, who use the camera as a fountain pen. One of them, Robert Bresson, wrote this of his work:

> Acting is for the theatre, which is a bastard art. The film can be true art because in it the author takes fragments of reality and arranges them in such a way that their juxta-position transforms them. Art *is* transformation. Each shot is like a word, which means nothing by itself, or rather means so many things that in effect it is meaningless. But a word in a poem is transformed, its meaning made precise and unique, by its placing in relation to the words around it; in the same way a shot in a film is given its meaning by its context, and each shot modifies the meaning of the previous one until with the last shot a total, unparaphrasable meaning has been arrived at. Acting has nothing to do with that, it can only get in the way. Films can be made only by by-passing the will of those who appear in them, using not what they do but what they are.[1]

An indication of the director's control over the finished work is not only in his command of cameramen and actors while shooting takes place, but in the cutting room afterwards, where, in a very real sense, the film is *made*.

[1] Ibid., p. 116

A discussion therefore of the art of the cinema could be based on the work of the directors. In what sense, so far as this present book is concerned, do they present a religious interpretation of life in their work? We might take three outstanding film-makers of recent years and compare their attitudes: Bergman, Bresson and Bunuel.

These three men, from Sweden, France and Spain respectively, reveal in their moral weight and seriousness the Christianity which formed them, and in their films they pose those questions which religion exists to answer. Bergman makes a tortured pilgrimage in a search for the meaning of God's purpose in our lives. His films are often filled with pain of the most acute kind, the pain which comes from our inability to co-exist in society without savaging each other. They have an elaborate and at times contrived symbolism and often use brutality, sexual per-version, and cruelty to make their points. In *The Seventh Seal* (1956), he takes up the theme of the relations of man with God and with death, setting this morality play in the middle ages, with the adventures of a knight and his squire as they make their way home across a plague-ravaged country to the castle and the inevitable final reckoning with death. Bergman has more recently com-pleted a loose trilogy of *Through a Glass Darkly*, *Winter Light*, and *The Silence*, which is also concerned with this theme: Does God exist? If he exists, what is he like? The schizophrenic Karen in the first of these films sees God finally as a monstrous spider on the wall. Is Bergman saying that God is no more than a figment of the diseased mind? Or does he hint, by the faint glimmers of hope, at a still centre of a world where love will be undefiled by the cruelty which surrounds us?

Bresson's characters endure their pain alone, for Bresson seems preoccupied with the scapegoat, with the innocent or would-be innocent (often a child or a priest) who suffers and dies to atone for the sins of the society in which he lives. His considerable reputation (although his films have hardly been popular successes) rests on the six films he has made in twenty years. His style is not easy, and his films have a quality of remoteness which limits their appeal. Perhaps his greatest film is *Le Journal d'un Curé de Campagne* (1950), based on the novel *Diary of a Country Priest*, by Georges Bernanos. It is a film which well illustrates the principles of film making quoted from Bresson earlier. Everything fits perfectly together, and the story is told with absolute economy and simplicity as the young priest moves through his hostile and unfriendly parish and his dark night of the soul; the French countryside is as cruel and remorseless as the cancer which ravages his body; yet at the end the priest is able to see a purpose in his life and dies with the words, 'Tout est grâce,' on his lips. 'Nothing in Bresson's work,' writes one critic, 'shows his mastery so completely as the conception and placing of the episode when, at his departure from Ambricourt, the Curé rides pillion on a motor-bike, the one sunny moment in an overcast, drizzling world, and for a short space of time we see him as he might have been in other circumstances; we see how far he is just like all other young men, and how, too, he is fundamentally, irrevocably different.'[1]

It seems strange to link Bresson and Bunuel since there could be no harsher contrast between the country priest of Bresson's films and the corrupt sensual priests who

[1] Ibid., p. 128

crowd the screen in Bunuel's work. Luis Bunuel was brought up in Catholic Spain, though he has made most of his films in Mexico. His *L'Age d'Or* shocked the 1930 audiences with its concentrated attack on the Church and the Establishment. It was, technically, well in advance of its time in its use of the sound-track, and it made the same sort of impact that *The Waste Land* had made eight years earlier in the world of letters. It was not dissimilar in theme from Eliot's poem for it portrayed a world where love is barren and society rootless. But it also shocked because it was not merely an attack against the abuses of a corrupt church, it was an attack on Christianity itself, with the Christ-figure an embodiment of evil.

Thirty years later Bunuel was still shocking the world with films like *Nazarin* and *Viridiana*, but the message is not so anarchistic as in his first work. *Nazarin* is, like Bresson's *Journal*, the story of a priest, a saintly priest. The priest is not ridiculed, as might have happened in earlier films; he is accepted as an heroic and saintly character. But despite this, his position is impossible because, for Bunuel, ideal Christianity is impossible. He himself remarked, 'One can be *relatively* Christian, but the absolutely pure being, the innocent, is condemned to defeat. He is beaten in advance.' As the priest tries to live a perfect Christian life he becomes misunderstood and rejected, an outcast from his own church and people; in the end he is saved from despair and brought to new hope by a disinterested act of kindness, the gift of a piece of fruit to a solitary man on a hot and lonely road. *Viridiana* continues to explore the life of the Christian and his purity of motive in an evil world. The Christian viewer may find it more destructive in tone than *Nazarin* and many would feel that the sequence in which a group of rogues gather round a table in a cruel parody of the Last Supper is offensive. Yet those who are offended ought to ask why Bunuel makes films like this. If, in his passionate attack on all that degrades human life—reaction, exploitation, superstition and falsehood—an attack on the Church is included, could it not be that there are grounds for this? And just because his personal philosophy is atheistic, Bunuel forces us to ask ultimate questions about the place and purpose of Christianity in modern life.

This study of the work of individual film-makers is one way of looking at films which pose basic and ultimate questions. Another method might be to examine films in certain categories and see how different attitudes to war, social injustice, personal relationships and the Church are subjected to scrutiny.

Twentieth century art has been forced to deal with war. Many artists have been directly involved in the two major wars of the century. These two conflicts are linked together in Britten's *War Requiem*, written initially to be performed in the cathedral at Coventry which arose out of the ashes of the second world war, and in which the poetry of Wilfred Owen, from the first world war, is set against the timeless words of the Latin Requiem. Picasso's *Guernica* grew out of the total reaction of a great artist to the wanton bombing of villages in the Spanish civil war. Rouault's *Miserere* prints, Reg Butler's *Political Prisoner*, and Remarque's *All Quiet on the Western Front*, are alike a protest against the horror and brutality of war and its degradation of man. The representation of war in the cinema is somewhat ambivalent. There are the many films that have glamourized war, presenting it as exciting adventure, bringing out heroism and leadership, without ever raising the basic questions about the purpose or futility of it all. If such questions are raised, usually tentatively in the closing minutes with the slaughter mounting, the heroic answer is given with stiff upper-lip and half-closed eyes, looking into the middle distance. In 633 *Squadron*, when almost all the pilots have been killed in a desperate mission, the Air Marshal who has been directing the operation with a stern disregard for human feelings is mildly rebuked by a younger officer—'And what have we achieved, sir? We've destroyed the whole squadron.' 'No,' he replies, lower jaw thrust forward, eyes on the horizon, 'You can't destroy a squadron.' And the music swells to a triumphant and martial conclusion.

One of the deficiencies of the average British war film is its lack of concern for the characters as genuine people. The officers are expected, naturally, to do their duty, which involves putting on a brave front and an implacable exterior which are supposed to conceal great reserves of strength. The other ranks invariably remain cheerful in all circumstances, with either a cockney or north-country accent, except for the one or two emotionally unstable men whom we know will crack up when the crisis comes. These weaknesses are not absent even from a film which purported to make serious statements about war. *Bridge on the River Kwai* was to some extent a conventional account of British military nonchalance and steadfastness, with the English Colonel Nicholson (played by Alec Guiness) gaining the upper hand in his moral battle with the Japanese commandant of the camp. It is true that there was a basic irony in the distorted values which 'doing the job properly' produced, so that the colonel becomes so

proud of the bridge as a token of the efficiency and spirit
of his men, that he is prepared to prevent its being blown
up by a group of British commandos. But the cry of
'Madness! Madness!' which the medical officer utters at
the end of the film does not achieve, in the context, the
strong indictment of war which the original book carried,
and as the final scene of senseless destruction fades from
the screen the strains of 'Colonel Bogey' carry, perhaps,
more than a faint hint of triumph.

If one wishes to see a sensitive, yet at the same time
ruthless, exposure of the inhumanity of war, one must go
to the Polish trilogy of Anton Wajda—*A Generation*, *Kanal*
and *Ashes and Diamonds*. These three films have been
shown on television and so have reached a wider audience
than many foreign films. Seen in that order they present
a kaleidoscope of the war as it affected the younger
generation in Poland. The first, not without some ideo-
logical traces of its Marxist origins, shows the impact of
the German occupation on a young Polish patriot and his
girl; the second is a hideous picture of the struggle for
survival in the sewers of Warsaw; and the third shows the
bitterness and disillusion which come at the end of the
war with the realization that those who take the sword
will perish by the sword. *A Generation* aptly illustrates the
difference between the commercial war film, action-packed
in glorious technicolour, but a film in no way threatening
or involving us; and a film made in black and white with
a limited budget and few, if any, star actors. The central
incident of the film seems almost trivial—a boy growing
into manhood in wartime Poland and discovering the real
cost of heroism. Yet in Wajda's hands this episode

escalates into a statement about Man and the film becomes a genuine affirmation of hope in a context of despair.

From quite a different ethos is *The Burmese Harp*, made in Japan. This dwells not on the horrors of war as they happen but on their effect on one man, a soldier, who is so disturbed by the suffering he has seen that he makes a pilgrimage of penance and becomes a monk. And to remind us that the war ended with the devastation of the Bomb, *Hiroshima Mon Amour* links in an imaginative, though to some an irritating, manner the memories of a French film star who is visiting Hiroshima to make a propaganda film, and who had had an affair with a local German soldier during the Occupation and had been ostracized by her village for it.

It cannot escape our notice how often in such films there is an unsympathetic attitude to the organized church. In *A Generation*, the boy attends a class at a Catholic seminary. He doesn't even know the Creed, but in his desperate situation, looking for leadership and help, all that the priest can mouth are the set ritual phrases which are greeted with titters from the rest of the class. Only a few moments later in the film there is a moving scene where the members of the local resistance group gather in an upper room. They stand in a circle, passing a cigarette from mouth to mouth and repeating their vows of loyalty. There is a religious intensity about that scene that makes us realize where Wajda's own sympathies lie. The Church has failed, and it is the Party which speaks to this generation.

One of the few genuine anti-war films to come from Great Britain is *King and Country*, made by Joseph Losey. The central character, a rather timid private who has 'deserted' after months in the trenches and is awaiting death, is visited by his comrades on the night before his dawn execution. They get him drunk, play blind man's buff with him and it is in this drunken state that he is discovered by the padre, who comes to administer Holy Communion to this uncomprehending 'innocent.' Again the words of the liturgy are spoken, prayers are said, and the elements are given, though the prisoner is immediately sick. Losey seems to be suggesting that this is what war does to man—it reduces him to the level of an animal (like the rats which the soldiers torture), and neither the concern of his fellow men nor the grace of God can be of any use.

Despite this hostility and the occasional caricature of the Church, films of this kind can never be dismissed as 'irreligious.' They could be regarded as presentations in contemporary terms of that moment on Calvary when our Lord cried: My God, My God, why hast thou forsaken me?

Another field in which the cinema has a wealth of comment to make is that of the relationship of individuals to society. *Shadows* and *The Defiant Ones* deal with the problem of colour; *Rocco and his Brothers* shows what happens when Italian peasants from the south move to hostile Milan in the industrial north; *La Dolce Vita* is surely a morality play about the vices of our wealthy society and its power to corrupt those who submit to it, with the dead, disapproving eye of the great stranded fish on the beach, putting Marcello properly in his place at the end. *The Angry Silence* condemns the tyranny of industrial conditions which refuse to a man his right to make his own protest and witness; *West Side Story* reveals the tension of gang warfare in the concrete jungle and the healing power of love; and *The Loneliness of the Long Distance Runner* hits hard at the 'Establishment society' which fails to understand its delinquents and which uses people as things—in this instance as animals to win the annual cross country race for the glory of the governor of the local Borstal.

A film which could be included in this group, yet which has a distinctive religious theme is *On the Waterfront* made in 1955 by Elia Kazan. Marlon Brando played Terry Malloy, a young ex-boxer who becomes involved with his brother's gang, led by Johnny Friendly who controls the labour force on the New York waterfront. Terry is partly responsible for the murder of an informer by the gang and the film is mainly concerned with the pressures of loyalty which Edie, the murdered man's sister with whom Terry falls in love, and Father Barry, a tough extrovert Catholic priest, bring to bear on him. There is loyalty to the unwritten code of the waterfront that nobody 'rats'; there is loyalty to his brother, threatened, and eventually killed, by the gang if Terry informs to the committee of inquiry into labour conditions, and there is loyalty to a conscience which is being slowly awakened by the girl and the priest. 'You're asking me to put my finger on my own brother,' Terry tells the priest. 'Well, you've got some other brothers and they're getting the short end.' Finally, Terry does give evidence and in the closing sequence of the film is brutally beaten up by Johnny Friendly and his gang. But he staggers to his feet, having in effect smashed the power of the gang and leads his workmates into the unloading bays, along his own Via Dolorosa. The film is a setting of a passion story in the industrial jungle, and at one point when another 'informer' has been deliberately crushed in the hold by an 'accident,' the priest preaches a 'sermon' over the body. The Passion of Christ continues in the death of this man—'You're all brothers in Christ, yet the love of a lousy buck rules the dock, not the love of Man.' *On the Waterfront* is not without its faults, both in technique and content, but it presents the eternal theme of the suffering which arises when good meets evil in the world.

Yet a third and basic area which the cinema explores is that of personal relationships and the nature of love and pity. The Italian director Michelangelo Antonioni has stated that his only objective is to relate human experiences. 'If they are tragic, it's because I believe the tragic sentiment dominates all of contemporary life; even the irony that pervades Pop art is tragic. The old mechanisms don't fit in with the cadence of modern life. Scientific man lives in a different world from that of pre-scientific man, but we retain impossible dreams that belong to the past, and we are frightened because we can't create a life out of old longings . . . we are no longer capable of love, only a sort of shared pity.' And so in *La Notte* we watch a husband and wife exist side by side without love, and the tragedy is underlined in that they are not only incapable of loving each other, but also that they can love no one.

In the British film *A Kind of Loving* the same questions are asked, but with more hopeful answers. It is set in an industrial town, and Ingrid, a typist, and Victor, a draughtsman at the same factory, become passionately involved with each other and yet are unable to define or communicate this attraction. Do their feelings arise only from physical attraction? Is it lust or love? Is she trying to capture a reliable husband and settle for security in a cosy semi-detached house? Or is Victor guilty of using her purely for his own pleasure? When Ingrid becomes pregnant they get married and live for a time with her possessive mother. Victor feels he has been caught in a matriarchal web and leaves Ingrid. But his family persuade him to 'patch things up' and his happily married sister talks to him about the kinds of loving: 'I know what you wanted, Vic, it's what most people want, though they're not all conscious of it. They want the other half of themselves, the other person who will make them whole . . . and you can't *love* a person till you know him or her inside out; until you've lived with them and shared experience: sadness, joy, *living*—you've got to share living before you can find love. Being *in* love doesn't last, but you can find love to take its place.'[1] This quotation is taken from the novel by Stan Barstow on which the film was based and which carries on its title page a quotation from Bacon's *Essays*: 'But little do we perceive what solitude is, and how far it extendeth. For a crowd is not company, and faces are but a gallery of pictures, and talk a tinkling cymbal, where there is no love.'

So far we have not mentioned the films which deal with Biblical material. They can only form a minor section of this chapter because in so many cases they do not offer a religious interpretation of life. We have seen again and again that the Christian faith is most effectively communicated when it is seen in terms of contemporary society; most of the novels and plays which portray Jesus in a Palestinian setting, concentrate attention so closely on those historical details that the essential and eternal truth about

[1] *A Kind of Loving*, Stan Barstow (Penguin), p. 261–2

man and God is lost. The latest Hollywood life of Christ, *The Greatest Story Ever Told*, has been greeted with dismay by the critics for its boredom and 'inoffensiveness.' Both this film and the earlier *King of Kings* give the effect of picturesque tableaux, and deferential reverence towards the person of a Christ who never challenges and disturbs men as did the real Jesus. But the desire not to offend any of the Christian denominations and even those of other faiths has a paralysing effect on the finished epic. 'Admirably restrained, supremely reverent, in very good taste, but dead,' was one verdict. Unfortunately Hollywood, assumes that the film with the largest cast, widest screen and highest budget will be the most effective. One of their official 'hand-outs' informs us that '*The Greatest Story ever Told* is being presented in the only way befitting such a subject on the giant Cinerama living screen. Supported by dozens of great star artists plus thousands of the populace, a mighty religious epic was produced that must be ageless and stand the test of repetition for decades to come. It was decided that no expense must be spared to perfect such a subject, and the final cost exceeded twenty million dollars.' It is ironic that at the same time that this multi-million dollar ultra-panavision epic was being screened in London, there was also on view Pasolini's *Gospel of St. Matthew*, a black and white film made on an economy budget by an Italian Marxist which presents far more effectively the drama and mystery of the Passion.

Hollywood seems happier with Old Testament subjects and *Samson and Delilah*, *David and Bathsheba*, *The Ten Commandments*, and *Barabbas* are constant evidence that religion, romance, and cruelty, plus an unlimited budget, make for commercial success, if not for artistic integrity.

There is a strange contrast between the spiritual grandeur which it is the purpose of these films to portray and the material grandiosity with which they are almost invariably realized. And there is often an undisguised exploitation of violence. A critic suggested that there was more violence in *Barabbas* than in any other picture he could name. In that particular film the violence was of an extreme kind— the viewer was never allowed to get away with *one* blow, or a *short* glimpse of a man being dragged behind a chariot. Burning, branding, eyes being taken out with hot irons seem to be the stock in trade of the Biblical epic film maker.

It is offensive that such resources and technical skill should be squandered on works which more often than not reveal ignorance and superstition, and combine banality of thought with vulgarity of intention. They purport to be 'religious' because the romantic and sadistic elements are sandwiched with snippets of ethical teaching or the singing of a celestial choir. These phoney 'religious' tit-bits are supposed to be giving the film its 'message' so that many of the audience will go home with a self-righteous glow which is utterly alien from the spirit not only of Christianity but of every great religion. This, fundamentally, is why they are not religious films, as are many listed elsewhere in this chapter.

9. Epilogue

SINS OF omission are inevitable in what is, for its subject, such a short book. But this book sets out to be no more than an introduction, and success can only be claimed if it leads its readers to explore for themselves the world of the arts. If we are truly to understand Art we must look at the novels, the plays, the paintings, the buildings and the musical compositions themselves. For Art is not merely a leisure-time diversion, a pleasant affectation indulged in by those who would escape from the harsh everyday world. The subject matter of Art is life, the human condition, the whole world about us. Its range is universal, there is nothing it does not touch. Sir Arthur Quiller-Couch once reminded his students at Cambridge that:

> The acknowledged masterpieces of English literature are great because they are alive, and traffic not with cold celestial certainties, but with men's hopes, aspirations, doubts, loves, hates, breakings of the heart; and the glory of beauty, the capricious uncertain lease on which you and I hold life, the dark coast to which we inevitably steer; all that amuses or vexes, all that gladdens, saddens, maddens us men and women on this brief and mutable traject which yet must be home for a while, the anchorage of our hearts.

Art, in this sense, is the response we make to our human predicament. It is man's effort to make his mark on this 'brief and mutable traject,' to enrich our human existence. And it is because of this enriching power that Art is never to be thought of in any narrow way as being concerned only with 'cold, celestial certainties' in the conventional religious sense.

Indeed, the definition of Art as 'anything well-made' should make us realize that we are concerned and involved in 'art' in our whole environment. There is a beauty of form and function in a piece of delicate and complex machinery like a Rolls-Royce aero engine, as well as in a Bach Fugue; there can be ugliness or beauty in the design of a car, no less than in that of a cathedral. And so our continuing journey into Art will not only involve us in thinking about 'works of art' but also about attitudes of taste, judgment of style and discrimination in every aspect of our daily life—in the way we furnish our homes, decorate our classrooms, design our cities. In this discrimination both form and content are important. For in any work of art the craftsmanship, the making, is an integral part of the finished thing. When writing is involved it is not just what is said, but the way that it is said that is important. So Gerald Vann maintains that 'good writing is part of truth. If you take a true proposition and state it in a sentimental way, in a sectarian way, in a vulgar way, you damage the truth of it.' It is ugliness that is the sin, the imperfection of form and content. That is why it is to be regretted that the Church has often had a monopoly of the tawdry and shoddy in its decorative art and furnishings.

This book began with a reference to the twin doctrines of Creation and Incarnation which are fundamental to the Christian faith and to a Christian understanding of art. It was the second of these doctrines that Eric Gill

L

had in mind when he described every work of art as being, in its way, an incarnation:

> What is a work of art? A word made flesh. That is the truth, in the clearest sense of the text. A word, that which emanates from the mind. Made flesh, a thing seen, a thing known, the immeasurable translated into the measurable.

Because of the other Incarnation, when the Word became flesh and the holy was rooted in the earth, the Christian artist works with the materials of earth, never being false to the realities of human experience yet at the same time revealing a meaning that is more than merely the material.

We have seen that for all artists in the modern world there are acute problems which arise because of the decay of symbolism and break-up of traditional forms. Yet there are some who have seen, and declared their vision:

> The world is aflame with the splendour of God
> It will flame out, like shining from shook foil.

The Christ-figures of Rouault speak of the terrible Grace of God, at work in a world so dominated by evil, just as his clowns express the pathos of our human existence, which only that Grace can redeem. The familiar images may have been broken, the plaster saints and madonnas shattered, but the Incarnate energy of God's eternal love can again, as before, make the very stones of our common experience cry out His praises.

Bibliography

This list includes books used in the preparation of this work and suggestions for further reading. In general, collections of the work of individuals have not been cited, and where possible the paperback edition has been given. Publishers marked * are British.

1. GENERAL: Culture, Aesthetics, Symbolism

Beardsley, M. C. *Aesthetics* Harcourt, Brace and World

Bridge, A. C. *Images of God* Hodder and Stoughton *

Coggin, P. A. *Art, Science, and Religion* Harrap *

Cope, G. *Symbolism in the Bible and the Church* Student Christian Movement Press *

Cope, G. (ed.) *Christianity and the Visual Arts* Faith Press *

Dillistone, F. W. *Christianity and Symbolism* Collins *

Glendenning, F. J. (ed.) *The Church and the Arts* Allenson

Jarrett-Kerr, M. *The Secular Promise* Fortress

Langer, S. *Feeling and Form* Scribner's

Malraux, A. *The Metamorphosis of the Gods* Doubleday

—— *The Voices of Silence* Doubleday

Maritain, J. *Creative Intuition in Art and Poetry* Meridian

Mumford, L. *Art and Technics* Columbia University Press

Roberts, M. *The Modern Mind* Faber *

Tillich, P. *Theology and Culture* Oxford University Press

Van der Leeuw *Sacred and Profane Beauty* Holt, Rinehart and Winston

Wilson, J. (ed.) *The Faith of an Artist* Allen and Unwin *

2. PAINTING AND SCULPTURE

Bazin, G. *Concise History of Art* Thames and Hudson *
Bowness, A. *Modern Sculpture* Dutton
Brion, M. *The Bible in Art (O. T.)* Phaidon
Du Bourguet, P. *Early Christian Painting* Viking
Gill, E. *Art* John Lane, Bodley Head *
Godfrey, F. M. *Christ and the Apostles* Studio Publications *
Gombrich, E. H. *Art and Illusion* Pantheon
—— *The Story of Art* Phaidon
Jobé, J. *Ecce Homo: the Christ of All the World* Macmillan *
Lowrie, W. *Art in the Early Church* Harper and Row
Morey, C. R. *Christian Art* Oldbourne Press
Newton, E. *The Arts of Man* New York Graphic
—— *European Painting and Sculpture* Barnes and Noble
Read, H. *The Meaning of Art* Penguin
—— *The Philosophy of Modern Art* Meridian
Ross, M. *The Life of Christ in Masterpieces of Art* Parrish *
Seuphor, M. *The Sculpture of this Century* Zwemmer *
Talbot-Rice, D. *The Beginnings of Christian Art* Hodder and Stoughton *
—— *Byzantine Art* Penguin
Visser 't Hooft, W. A. *Rembrandt and the Gospel* Westminster
Weidlé, W. *The Dilemma of the Arts* Student Christian Movement Press *
Wilenski, R. H. *The Modern Movement in Art* Boston Book and Art Shop
Wilson, W. *Christian Art Since the Romantic Movement* Burns and Oates *

3. ARCHITECTURE

Biéler, A. *Architecture in Worship* Westminster
Clark, K. *The Gothic Revival* Holt, Rinehart and Winston

Hammond, P. *Liturgy and Architecture* Columbia University Press

Hammond, P. (ed.) *Towards a Church Architecture* Architectural Press *

Kidder-Smith, G. E. *The New Churches of Europe* Holt, Rinehart and Winston

—— *New Architecture of Europe* Penguin

Le Corbusier *Towards a New Architecture* Praeger

Lockett, W. *The Modern Architectural Setting of the Liturgy* SPCK *

Mâle, É. *The Gothic Image* Harper Torchbook

Mills, E. D. *The Modern Church* Architectural Press *

Mumford, L. *The Culture of Cities* Harcourt, Brace and World

Murray, K. and Maguire, R. *Modern Churches of the World* Dutton

Nellist, J. B. *British Architecture and its Background* Macmillan *

Pevsner, N. *Outline of European Architecture* Penguin

Rasmussen, S. E. *Experiencing Architecture* M. I. T. Press

Richards, J. M. *An Introduction to Modern Architecture* Barnes and Noble

—— *The Chapel at Ronchamp* Architectural Press *

Simson, O. von *The Gothic Cathedral* Harper Torchbook

Spence, B. *Phoenix at Coventry* Fontana *

Wittkower, R. *Architectural Principles in the Age of Humanism* Random House

4. MUSIC

Cleall, C. *Music and Holiness* Epworth *

Douglas, W. *Church Music in History and Practice* Scribner's

Dunwell, W. *Music and the European Mind* Jenkins *

Harmon, A. and others *Man and His Music* Oxford University Press

Mellers, W. *Music and Society* Dover

Northcott, C. *Hymns in Christian Worship* Lutterworth *

Routley, E. *Church Music and Theology* Fortress

—— *The Church and Music* Allenson

—— *Twentieth Century Church Music* Oxford University Press

Smallman, B. *The Background of Passion Music* Allenson

5. FICTION

Allen, W. *The English Novel* Dutton

Allott, K. and Farris, M. *The Art of Graham Greene* Russell and Russell (Atheneum)

Allott, M. (ed.) *Novelists on the Novel* Columbia University Press

Brooks, C. *The Hidden God* (Studies in Hemingway, Faulkner, Eliot, Yeats, and Warren) Yale University Press

Dillistone, F. W. *The Novelist and the Passion Story* Sheed and Ward

Fraser, G. S. *The Modern Writer and His World* Penguin

Gindin, J. *Post-War British Fiction* University of California Press

Jarrett-Kerr, M. *D. H. Lawrence and Human Existence* Allenson

Karl, F. R. *Reader's Guide to the Contemporary English Novel* Noonday

Kettle, A. *An Introduction to the English Novel* (2 vols.) Harper Torchbook

Leavis, F. R. *D. H. Lawrence: Novelist* Knopf

Mueller, W. R. *The Prophetic Voice in Modern Fiction* Association

Scott, N. A. *Rehearsals of Discomposure* (Studies in Kafka, Silone, Lawrence, and Eliot) Columbia University Press

Scott, N. A. (ed.) *The Tragic Vision and the Christian Faith* Association

Stewart, D. *The Ark of God* (Studies in five modern novelists) Carey Kingsgate Press*

Turnell, M. *Modern Literature and Christian Faith* Newman

Wilder, A. *Theology and Modern Literature* Harvard University Press

6. POETRY

Barnes, K. *The Creative Imagination* Humanities Press

Blackmur, R. P. *Language as Gesture* Allen and Unwin *

Bodkin, M. *Archetypal Patterns in Poetry* Oxford University Press

Brooks, C. *The Well-Wrought Urn* Harcourt, Brace and World

—— *Modern Poetry and the Tradition* Oxford University Press

Cohen, J. M. *Poetry of this Age* Hutchinson *

Daiches, D. *The Present Age in British Literature* Indiana University Press

Eliot, T. S. *On Poetry and Poets* Noonday

Empson, W. *Seven Types of Ambiguity* New Directions

Every, G. *Poetry and Personal Responsibility* Student Christian Movement Press *

Frye, R. M. *God, Man and Satan* Princeton University Press

Lewis, C. Day *The Poetic Image* Oxford University Press

McGill, A. C. *The Celebration of Flesh* Association

Matthiessen, F. O. *The Achievement of T. S. Eliot* Oxford University Press

Morgan, K. E. *Christian Themes in Contemporary Poets*
    Student Christian Movement Press *
Sansom, C. (ed.) *The World of Poetry* Writer
Thompson, D. *Reading and Discrimination* Hillary House
Wilson, E. *Axel's Castle* Scribner's
Wimsatt, W. K. *The Verbal Ikon* University of Kentucky
    Press

7. DRAMA

Aylen, L. *Greek Tragedy and the Modern World* Methuen *
Baxter, K. M. *Speak What We Feel* Student Christian
    Movement Press *
Brustein, R. *The Theatre of Revolt* Little, Brown and Co.
Chiari, J. *Landmarks of Contemporary Drama* Interna-
    tional Publications Service
Esslin, M. *The Theatre of the Absurd* Doubleday Anchor
Frye, R. M. *Shakespeare and Christian Doctrine* Princeton
    University Press
Lumley, F. *Trends in Twentieth Century Drama* Oxford
    University Press
Merchant, W. M. *Creed and Drama* Fortress
Taylor, J. R. *Anger and After* Penguin
Williams, R. *Drama from Ibsen to Eliot* Oxford Univer-
    sity Press

8. CINEMA

Bergman, I. *Four Screenplays* Simon and Schuster
Eisenstein, S. *Film Form* Harcourt, Brace and World
—— *Film Form and the Film Sense* Meridian
Houston, P. *The Contemporary Cinema* Penguin
Kracauer, S. *Theory of Film* Oxford University Press
Leyda, J. *Kino: A History of the Russian and Soviet Film*
    Allen and Unwin *

Manvell, R. *Film* Penguin
—— *The Living Screen* Harrap *
Mayer, J. P. *The Sociology of Film* Faber *
Montagu, I. *Film World* Penguin
Stephenson, R. and Debrix, J. R. *The Cinema as Art*
Penguin
Taylor, J. R. *Cinema Eye, Cinema Ear* Hill and Wang

9. POPULAR CULTURE

Hoggart, R. *The Uses of Literacy* Beacon
Thompson, D. (ed.) *Discrimination and Popular Culture*
Penguin
Lynch, W. F. *The Image Industries* Sheed and Ward
Whannell, P. and Hall, S. *The Popular Arts* Pantheon
Williams, R. *Culture and Society, 1780-1950* Harper and
Row
—— *The Long Revolution* Columbia University Press

Index

This index includes the names of those whose work is mentioned in the text and the titles of those works about which there is some discussion.